My Dinner
with Lawrence

RECIPES AND DINNER PARTIES
INSPIRED BY NOTABLE ARCHITECTS

A Project of the Tulane
School of Architecture
Class of 1980-81

WITH THANKS TO

All the classmates who helped create this book

Chris Thomas for being our beta model

Virginia Walcott for herding all of the cats

Errol Barron for sharing his thoughts about John Lawrence

Kate Barron for her thoughtful edits

DEDICATED TO

Linda Lawlor, Jorge Rodriguez, Kurt Hoffman, Dave Bien,
and James Davis; our classmates who are no longer with us.

PREFACE

When Mac Walcott asked me about writing a few notes for a preface to this book, my first thought was to say something primarily about the class of '80, whose emergence onto the scene at the Tulane School of Architecture coincided roughly with my own beginnings there as a young faculty member.

When the class of '80 arrived in New Orleans, I had only been at Tulane for a year and was thrown in with this class in a number of ways quite apart from teaching. It was a very congenial and spirited group and we shared a number of interests such as cycling and drinking, but we also connected in the second year when I was assigned to this group as a studio instructor. Their exuberant collective spirit coincided nicely with the enthusiasms of a young faculty member fresh in from NYC and London. This was only my second teaching job, the previous one a one year stint in London, and I was full of excitement doing something I had hoped to do since being a student myself in the early 60's.

New ideas abounded; the nearly puritanical ethos of modernism was being questioned by leaders such as Chares Moore and Robert Venturi (my teachers in graduate school), and even though the permissiveness of post-modernism now seems like an indulgent diversion, it then seemed a promising set of liberating ideas. A reawakening and respect for history, an enthusiasm for existing buildings, grand and modest, as well as the elevation of "contextualism" to a near sacred state set the stage of our academic life.

All of that has gone thought numerous stages of evaluation, in recent years from a "rediscovery" of classic modernism to the inevitable incorporation of the computer and digital fabrication. It is hard to believe that this class did not know what a computer was except as an abstract idea. The class of '80 has lived through this complete cycle and somehow survived with a robust sense of humor (for the most part).

This esprit de corps to a large extent depended on the ideas of JOHN W. LAWRENCE, the beloved Dean of the School who died just before this class came to Tulane. Lawrence, as Dean, and as a respected prize-winning architect, was a leading figure in the preservation movement, believeing as he did in the value of historic buildings, especially in New Orleans where there were so many good buildings surviving from the past. New Orleans dodged the urban renewal bullet in a big way and remains as the most intact 18th-19th century city in America. This fact is in a large part traceable to Lawrence and his generation of architects, but especially him, in such monumentally important actions such as the stopping of the Riverfront Expressway that would have, in effect, destroyed the Vieux Carré.

At that time, when the Class of '80 began, New Orleans was still regarded a bit as a cultural backwater, quaint and irrelevant to the outside world (we knew differently). But as environmental and architectural awareness (and preservation) began to loom, New Orleans began to be looked to as a guide for the future. The Class of '80 was in the middle of this slowly-evolving reality.

The collaborative spirit of this class is evident in their assembling the following contributions in this book that is not only a collection of recipes for a food and pleasure-loving group, but forms a sort of loose record of the bizarre isolation we have all been enduring for six months – identified by 'social distancing,' a concept utterly foreign to the Class of '80.

Errol Barron
TUSA 1964

INTRODUCTION

In the Fall of 1975, fifty-seven of us arrived at Richardson Memorial and immediately began our cold-water immersion into the fantastical program known as the Tulane School of Architecture. We were 17-18 year old kids, strangers from all over; from Canton, OH; Princeton, NJ; San Bernadino, CA; Greenville, MS; Panama City, Panama; Chicago, Illinois; and Algiers, LA. We emerged from our Architectural Baptism five or six years later with our brains and hearts completely rebuilt and our eyes wide open to a new way of understanding the world. Bill Turner was our Dean then, and he proudly described his TUSA program as "the best Liberal Arts education you can find anywhere". And he was right. We took his blessings and scattered in many directions and became many things: architects, filmmakers, artists, Deans (three of them), farmers, parents, teachers, landscape architects, program managers, and writers, all springing from the TUSA font that Dean Turner called "the Queen of Arts."

Through all of this, we have created some wonderfully enduring relationships with each other over the last 45 years. As we prepare to celebrate our 40th class reunion, we've had a chance to talk and share memories of that amazing moment in time at TUSA that shapes us to this day. We have assembled this book to celebrate these relationships and memories.

The original version of this cookbook was baked during the Great Recession. There was very little architectural work to do then, so we formed Little House Publishing to produce local books and stories. We ended up making five smartphone apps and a great list of book concepts, including this one. Little House Publishing then went back on the shelf, as the architecture work came back.

The current version of this cookbook emerged in early 2020 from a Covid-induced email chain that included 15-20 of our classmates. In one of the emails, Scott Paden suggested we write a cookbook together. We quickly dusted off this concept from 2009, and here it is.

My Dinner with Lawrence is a Wiki-cookbook type of creation. Our classmates were each asked to pick their favorite architect, write a brief description of their work, and then imagine and illustrate that architect's favorite food and drink recipes. As a bonus, the classmates were then asked to do the same for their own work and favorite recipes. We also included some folks who weren't in our class, just to spice things up a bit.

It is our hope that this little book can inspire many of us to host a Calatrava cocktail party or a Borromini breakfast and continue to learn more about the "Queen of Arts" and the special world at TUSA that helped make this book. Proceeds from the publication of *My Dinner with Lawrence* will befit the TUSA 80/81 Fund, a vehicle created by our class to help support TUSA and the memories of the ones who taught us to see differently.

Mac Walcott, B. Arch TUSA 1980
Editor and Publisher

WHY THIS TITLE?

The Prytania Theater was popular in our class because of its Uptown location and its runs of newer art films and older classics. "What's playing at the Prytania?" would be a common out-loud question at night in the studio. Someone might then take a look at scattered pages of The Gambit, Hullabaloo, Figaro, Advocate, States Item, or Times Picayune that were always around, pre-internet. The campus station, WTUL, usually playing non-stop from one our little radios, might also answer our question.

One night in 1981, a gaggle of us went to see *My Dinner with Andre* at the Prytania. It was a Louis Malle comedy-drama about two old friends who meet for a long dinner in Manhattan and talk about the nature of life, humanism, and their spiritual experiences. It was a wonderful film, and many of us came away humbled by it because the film gave a forecast of the many issues we would soon be consumed by as we left the TUSA bubble and entered the "real world" that many of us so dreaded.

In choosing the title of our cookbook, we were inspired by the film and the image of a special meal that Errol Barron and John Lawrence might have had, and the dreams of cooking a great meal together with our old friends, when we meet again.

NOTABLE ARCHITECT	TULANE CONTRIBUTOR	

NOTABLE ARCHITECT

Abbey of Fontenay

BURGUNDY, FRANCE
COMPLETED CIRCA 1118

TULANE CONTRIBUTORS

Beth Ganser and
Jerry Colomb

TUSA 1980/81

Tucked away in the agrarian hills and valleys of Burgundy, **ABBEY OF FONTENAY** is ideally suited to its time and place. Founded by an order of Cistercian monks, it embodies the austerity of its inhabitants – "to work is to pray."

Cistercian architecture followed simple principles that perfectly encapsulate its use – a place for monks to worship, live, and work. Even the names of the spaces seem to follow this utilitarian rule – Cloister, Sacristy, Common Room, Warming Room, Dovecote, Dormitory, Infirmary, Forge, Bakery. It is more an expression of a way of life than a singular vision.

We'll let the pictures tell the story – pure, logical forms, materials and surfaces that become more beautiful with age, human scale. And the light – how to describe it? Bernard of Clairvaux eschewed high ornamentation and imagery, believing that only light should enter the church. Now a UNESCO World Heritage site, this is an architectural pilgrimage par excellence.

- Beth Ganser and Jerry Colomb (TUSA 1980/81)

RIGHT AND ABOVE: THE CLOISTERS AT ABBEY OF FONTENAY

Abbey of Fontenay | Dinner Party

MAIN COURSE
Pan-Fried Trout

DRINK
Chimay Gold Clone (Page 16)

SIDE DISH
Haricots Verts Dijon

Those self-sufficient monks were known for their expertise in water engineering. They built a water-powered forge and were skilled in metallurgy. They also had a trout pond, so get out your cast iron frying pan for some pan-fried trout. (Even better, catch a fresh trout and cook over an open fire).

- Beth Ganser and Jerry Colomb

TROUT POND, ABBEY OF FONTENAY

Haricots Verts Dijon

1 LB GREEN BEANS

3-4 TBSP OLIVE OIL

1 TBSP RED WINE VINEGAR

2 TSP WHOLE GRAIN DIJON MUSTARD

1 MINCED SHALLOT

SALT AND PEPPER

CAYENNE (OPTIONAL)

Boil a large pot of salted water. Add green beans and cook until they are bright green and crisp, about 1 minute. Drain and transfer the beans to a bowl of ice water. Let stand for 1 minute. Drain and spread beans on a towel to dry. Meanwhile, whisk together olive oil, red wine vinegar, whole grain Dijon mustard, and minced shallot in a bowl. Add the beans, season with salt & pepper, and toss to combine. Serve hot or cold.

Adapted from SAVEUR, June 8, 2015

Pan-Fried Trout

4 TROUT, DRESSED (6-8 OZ EACH)

1/2 CUP MILK

1/2 CUP CORNMEAL

2 TBSP BUTTER

2 TBSP VEGETABLE OIL

SALT AND BLACK PEPPER

CAYENNE (OPTIONAL)

Rinse fish and pat dry. Pour milk into a pie pan and spread some corn meal on a plate. Dip both sides of fish in the milk, let it drip, then roll in cornmeal and shake off excess. Space fish out on waxed paper or a plate. Sprinkle with salt, black pepper, and maybe a touch of cayenne.

In a pan, melt butter and oil over medium-high heat. Add fish and cook until crisp and browned on one side, 4-5 minutes. Using a spatula, gently turn and cook the 2nd side until that side is also crisp and the flesh is just opaque (gently open cavity to check), 5-6 minutes longer.

*Adapted from Williams-Sonoma Complete
Outdoor Living Cookbook*

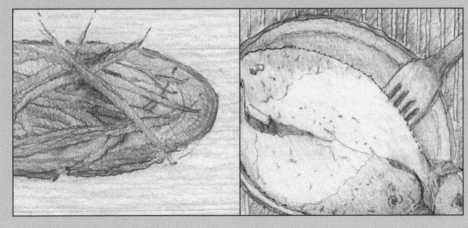

ILLUSTRATIONS BY BETH GANSER

Beth Ganser and Jerry Colomb (TUSA 1980/81)

Since graduation, we have lived and worked in North Yemen (2+ years), Chicago (17 years + 2 children), Denver (5 years + 2 dogs), Charlotte (5 years), and New England (2+ years). Jerry has been working (and Beth barely working) in the San Francisco Bay Area since 2014. With the exception of Yemen, all locations have had excellent biking!

FAVORITE RECIPE

Chimay Gold Clone Witbier (24 A)

We're pairing our trout with a Belgian ale, brewed in the Trappist tradition. We asked a family member who brews beer to create a recipe, but you can also find Chimay at better wine and liquor stores.

Type: All Grain
Batch Size: 12.00 gal
Boil Size: 14.80 gal
Boil Time: 60 min
Final Bottling Vol: 11.00 gal
Fermentation: Ale, Two Stage

Date: 07 Sep 2020
Brewer: Avery Colomb
Equipment: My HERMs
Efficiency: 90.00 %
Est Mash Efficiency: 91.9 %
Taste Rating: 30.0

Ingredients

9 lbs	Pilsen (Dingemans) (1.6 SRM)	Grain	1	58.1%	0.70 gal
6 lbs 8 oz	White Wheat Malt (2.4 SRM)	Grain	3	41.9%	0.51 gal
2.00 oz	Saaz [3.75 %] - Boil 60.0 min	Hop	6	13.1 IBUs	- - - - -
1.00 oz	Hallertau [4.50 %] - Boil 15.0 min	Hop	7	3.9 IBUs	- - - - -
2.00 oz	Orange Peel, Bitter (Boil 5.0 mins)	Spice	8	- - - - -	- - - - -
1.00 oz	Coriander Seed (Boil 5.0 mins)	Spice	9	- - - - -	- - - - -
3.0 pkg	Trappist Ale (White Labs #WLP500) [35.49 ml]	Yeast	10	- - - - -	- - - - -

Gravity, Alcohol Content and Color

Est Original Gravity: 1.041 SG
Est Final Gravity: 1.007 SG
Estimated Alcohol by Vol: 4.9 %
Bitterness: 17.0 IBUs
Est Color: 2.8 SRM

Measured Original Gravity: 1.046 SG
Measured Final Gravity: 1.010 SG
Actual Alcohol by Vol: 4.7 %
Calories: 151.6 kcal/12oz

Mash Profile

Mash Name: RIMS-HERMS Single Infusion, Light Body
Sparge Water: 10.75 gal
Sparge Temperature: 168.0 F
Adjust Temp for Equipment: FALSE Est Mash PH: 5.71
Measured Mash PH: 5.72

Total Grain Weight: 15 lbs 8.0 oz
Grain Temperature: 72.0 F
Tun Temperature: 72.0 F
Target Mash PH: 5.20
Mash Acid Addition: None Sparge
Acid Addition: None

Mash Steps

Mash In: Add 24.37 qt of water at 157.9 Fn
Mash Out: Heat to 168.0 F over 10 min168.0 F10 min
Sparge: Fly sparge with 10.57 gal water at 168.0 F
Mash Notes: Simple single infusion mash for use with most modern well modified grains (about 95% of the time). Uses infusion for first mash step and direct RIMS/HERMS heat to reach mash out temp.

Carbonation and Storage

Carbonation Type: Bottle
Pressure/Weight: 8.64 oz
Keg/Bottling Temperature: 70.0 F
Fermentation: Ale, Two Stage
Storage Temperature: 65.0 F

Volumes of CO2: 2.3
Carbonation Est: Bottle with 8.64 oz Corn
Fermenter: Sugar
Carbonation (from Meas Vol): Bottle with 3.93 oz Corn Sugar
Age for: 30.00 days

Mimar Sinan

OTTOMAN EMPIRE
1490 - 1588

Catherine Wilkins

TUSA 1983

SULEYMANIYE MOSQUE COURTYARD (ISTANBUL, TURKEY) DESIGNED BY MIMAR SINAN

MIMAR SINAN was born in the Ottoman Empire around 1490 and was active from 1520 to 1588. His family was Christian, and he was given up as tribute sometime around age 18 to be converted to Islam, trained and educated, and conscripted into the Janissary Corps of the Ottoman Empire. He was appointed to his position as "Architect of the Abode of Felicity" in 1538, and died in 1588 (he held the position for 50 years and died around age 98!) He is credited with hundreds of buildings; mosques, bathhouses, medreses, palaces and pavilions, as well as public works such as aqueducts. As the chief architect, he designed the most important buildings erected by the Ottoman rulers during this period of enormous power and wealth of the Empire. His work is compared to that of Michelangelo, who was his contemporary. Classical Ottoman architecture has a relatively small vocabulary of elements; domes, arches, squares. Sinan's vision and skill combined and renewed these elements in fresh ways, imbuing the familiar with a sophistication and ethereal beauty to make the familiar beautiful and new. His body of work is enormous and his influence on Ottoman Architecture cannot be overstated.

- Catherine Wilkins (TUSA 1983)

SELIMIYE MOSQUE (EDIRNE, TURKEY) DESIGNED BY MIMAR SINAN

| Mimar Sinan | Dinner Party |

APPETIZER
Smoked Eggplant Dip

SOUP
Red Lentil Soup

MAIN DISH
Köfte (Turkish Meatballs)

DESSERT
Baklava*

A Turkish evening meal will typically start with multiple appetizers, called meze. Stuffed grape leaves, smoked eggplant dip, marinated beans, olives, borek pastries, hummus, shepard's salad, spicy tomato salad – there are so many possibilities. Then a soup course, followed by the main dish – think lamb, probably shish kebab – and for dessert perhaps a slice of watermelon or baklava. Finish with a Turkish coffee.

- Catherine Wilkins

Red Lentil Soup

2 CUPS RED LENTILS

1 TBSP OLIVE OIL

1 ONION, CHOPPED SMALL

1 CARROT, CHOPPED SMALL

2 TBSP TOMATO PASTE

SALT AND PEPPER TO TASTE

Brown the carrot and onion in the olive oil. Add remaining ingredients and water to cover everything. Your lentils should expand and dissolve into a mush. Add water or vegetable stock as needed.

Simmer gently for 30-40 minutes or until everything is soft. Use an immersion blender to smooth out any bits of carrot and onion.

This is traditionally served with a sprinkling of dried mint or sumac, that I consider optional, and non-optional squeezes of lemon juice that are absolutely delicious.

Smoked Eggplant Dip

2 1/2 LBS EGGPLANT

1/4 CUP PLAIN WHOLE MILK GREEK YOGURT

2 TBSP FRESHLY SQUEEZED LEMON JUICE

2 TBSP JULIENNED FRESH MINT LEAVES, PLUS EXTRA FOR SERVING

1 TBSP MINCED GARLIC

OLIVE OIL

1/2 TSP SRIRACHA

KOSHER SALT AND FRESHLY GROUND BLACK PEPPER

This recipe works best on a charcoal grill. Make a fire on one side. Once it's hot, prick the eggplants all over with a fork, and place them on the hot side of the grill for 10 minutes, turning occasionally, to char the skin all over. Transfer the eggplants to the cool side of the grill. With the vents open, replace the lid and roast the eggplants for 40 to 45 minutes. Turn once halfway through. Move the eggplants to a platter and cut in half lengthwise, allowing any liquid to run out.

Use a slotted spoon to scoop the insides of the eggplants into the bowl of a food processor. Discard skin and extra liquid. Add the yogurt, lemon juice, mint, garlic, 1 tablespoon olive oil, Sriracha, 2 teaspoons salt, and 1 teaspoon pepper. Pulse just five or six times to combine but not puree the ingredients.

Transfer to a shallow serving bowl. Drizzle with olive oil, extra mint, and salt. Serve with pita bread or vegetable spears.

Adapted from Ina Garten's "Cook Like a Pro"

Köfte (Turkish Meatballs)

8 OZ MINCED LAMB

1 RED ONION, FINELY CHOPPED

4 GARLIC CLOVES, CRUSHED WITH SALT

1 TBSP TOMATO SAUCE

1 TBSP PINE NUTS, CHOPPED

1 TBSP CURRANTS, SOAKED IN WATER AND CHOPPED

1-2 TSP CINNAMON

1/2 TSP RED PEPPER FLAKES

2 SLICES OF BREAD, RUBBED INTO CRUMBS

1 EGG

BIG BUNCH OF PARSLEY AND DILL, CHOPPED

SALT AND PEPPER

FLOUR AND OIL

In a bowl, pound the meat together with the onion and garlic. Add all the other ingredients then knead well to thoroughly mix together. Shape the mixture into small round balls. Flatten each ball and roll them in the flour. Heat a deep layer of oil in a frying pan and brown the köfte on all sides. Drain on paper towels and serve with lemon wedges and yogurt.

*Pick up some Baklava from your favorite bakery

TULANE CONTRIBUTOR

Catherine Wilkins (TUSA 1983)

My career path has been as a Construction Manager, working for various government agencies. In that capacity, I have spent a lot of time on construction sites and consider what I do as the most fun job ever. Before graduating from TUSA, I took time off and interned at a firm in Paris for about a year. After graduation, I worked in Alaska for a couple of years, then went into the Peace Corps in Honduras (yes I am trilingual). Returning to Alaska, I worked as a construction project manager for the Coast Guard, which sent me all over the state inspecting the construction of shore facilities. I then went to work at the US Department of State, working on construction of diplomatic facilities overseas. Highlights were projects in Bogota, Buenos Aires, Istanbul and Dushanbe (Tajikistan), where I was in charge of the construction of a new US Embassy building compound.

I returned to Alaska about 15 years ago and worked for the municipality of Juneau, overseeing the construction of a high school and public swimming pool as well as smaller renovation projects. For the last 6 years I've been at the State of Alaska Dept. of Transportation overseeing civil engineering works. Back in New Orleans in the late 70's I couldn't have predicted this long crazy career, but it's been fabulous.

Possibly my most memorable project was the renovation of the US Ambassador's Residence, also known as Palacio Bosch, in Buenos Aires, Argentina. The interior had just been done; I was there for about a year overseeing the restoration of the exterior. This involved working with specialists to repair, restore, and/or replace the faux stone plaster walls and decorative castings. The building itself is stupendous – when a bunch of US Senators came for lunch one day, Tom Daschle's wife said it made The White House look shabby.

FAVORITE RECIPE

Pasta Puttanesca

2 14-OZ CANS OF DICED TOMATOES

2 TBSP OLIVE OIL

2 CLOVES GARLIC (OR MORE)

2 TBSP CAPERS, RINSED AND DRAINED

3/4 CUP BLACK OLIVES

1 TBSP ANCHOVY PASTE - OPTIONAL

RED PEPPER FLAKES TO TASTE

BLACK PEPPER AND SALT TO TASTE

Put a big pot of water on to make the pasta. While that is heating up, make the sauce: put olive oil in a frying pan, then sauté the garlic for a few seconds and add the tomatoes. Mix in the capers, olives, red pepper, black pepper, and salt. Let that simmer while you cook the pasta. I like spaghetti with this sauce. When the pasta is done, the sauce is done – it's a very quick dish to make.

RIGHT: INTERIOR, SULEYMANIYE MOSQUE, DESIGNED BY MIMAR SINAN

NOTABLE ARCHITECT

Francesco Borromini

BISSONE, SWITZERLAND
1599 - 1667

TULANE CONTRIBUTOR

Frank Weiner

TUSA 1980

SANT'AGNESE CHURCH IN AGONE (PIAZZA NAVONA, ROME, ITALY) DESIGNED BY BORROMINI

FRANCESCO BORROMINI was born in what is today the village of Bissone in the modern Swiss canton of Ticino. His trade and craft-based knowledge as a stone mason enabled him to both conceive and realize works of great architectural complexity.

The two masterpieces of Borromini, both located in Rome, are the relatively small church complexes of San Carlo alle Quattro Fontane also known as San Carlino (begun in 1638 and completed after his death) and Sant'Ivo alla Sapienza (1642- 1660). They are among the finest Baroque works in all of Rome and visibly appear as analogical precursors to the complex form of the fugue heard in the music of Johann Sebastian Bach (1685-1750).

Borromini's sheer architectural talent was only equaled by the strong sway of his personal demons. He passed away as the result of the self-inflicted wounds of a failed suicide attempt. Borromini's tragic demise should not detract from acknowledging his virtuosity as an architect. As the Russian poet Joseph Brodsky reminds us, in the good practice of one's art, happiness does not always accrue.

One could say the interior spaces of these two churches capture in stone, brick, and plaster the movements and counter movements of a fugue-like architecture. In these two works, Borromini not only 'aspired to the condition of music,' but achieved the condition of music to the extent this may be possible in architecture.

- *Frank Weiner (TUSA 1980)*

CHURCH OF SANT'IVO ALLA SAPIENZA (ROME, ITALY) DESIGNED BY BORROMINI, PHOTO BY FRANK WEINER

Francesco Borromini | Dinner Party

APERTIVO
Acqua di Rose
*Organic rosewater flavored
with Malvasia Wine*

ANTIPASTI
Carciofi Alla Giudia
*Roman-Jewish deep-fried
artichokes*

MAIN COURSE
Bestila
*Sweet and savory squab and
almond pie, Moroccan style*

DOLCE
Pomegranate Gelato*
With espresso

DIGESTIVO
Hypoclas
A commercially available spiced liquior

POST-DINNER WALK
Location of your choice

Requires an ice cream maker

Carciofi Alla Giudia

Roman-Jewish Deep-Fried Artichokes

4 GLOBE ARTICHOKES, HEAVY AND FIRM WITH
COMPACT LEAVES
OLIVE OIL FOR FRYING

COARSE KOSHER SALT
4-5 FRESH LEMONS, HALVED, FOR PREPARATION
AND SERVING

Prepare a large bowl of ice water. Squeeze the juice of two of the lemons into the bowl of water; stir. Add the squeezed lemons to the bowl and set aside. Have remaining cut lemons, cut-side down, on a cutting board nearby.

Rinse artichokes under cold water. Pat them dry with paper towels. Using kitchen shears or a very large sharp knife, cut off an inch of the thorny tips from the leaves. Cut off a half-inch of the stem, and peel what remains. Dip artichokes into lemon water bath. Transfer to paper towels. Beginning at the top of the stem and working your way up the artichoke, break or peel off the outer leaves of the artichoke until you reach the light green, tenderer leaves. Dip artichokes in lemon water again before continuing.

With a serrated knife or sharp chef's knife, slice the artichoke horizontally about ¾- inch above the base (heart) to remove the pointy top of the artichoke, leaving a flat crown of leaves on the base of the artichoke while exposing the inner purple leaves.

Slice the artichoke in half lengthwise (or into quarters), splitting the stem and heart in half vertically to reveal the inner fuzzy choke. Scoop out the fuzzy spines and purple leaves from each artichoke half with a serrated grapefruit spoon or melon baller, leaving behind two hollowed out halves of heart, each with a small crown of flat leaves. Rub the artichokes well with a lemon half and then submerge them in lemon water while heating the oil.

In a deep, medium saucepan or deep fryer, heat at least 4 inches of olive oil to 220 degrees. Drain and pat dry with paper towels as many artichoke halves as will fit in your pot without touching each other.

Set a layer of paper towels near your pot. Carefully lower artichokes into the hot oil and fry for 12-15 minutes, or until they are tender when pricked with a fork. Using a slotted spoon or spider, lift artichokes onto the stack of paper towels, cut side down. When cool enough to handle, gently open leaves a bit.

Raise the heat of the oil to 375 degrees and lower half of the artichokes back into hot oil. Fry for an additional 30-45 seconds, or until crisp and deep brown, then lift out of oil with a slotted spoon onto paper towels.

Season the fried artichokes with plenty of coarse kosher salt. Repeat with remaining artichoke halves. Serve artichokes on small plates, garnished with lemon wedges.

Makes 4-8 appetizer servings.

Bestila

*Sweet and savory squab and almond pie,
Moroccan style*

1/4 CUP OLIVE OIL

2 MEDIUM ONIONS, PEELED AND FINELY CHOPPED

1 STICK CINNAMON

1 TSP GROUND GINGER

PINCHES SAFFRON THREADS

SALT AND FRESHLY GROUND WHITE PEPPER

2 1-LB SQUABS (SUBSTITUTE CAPON IF DESIRED)

3 TSP GROUND CINNAMON

4 TSP ORANGE-FLOWER WATER

2 EGGS, LIGHTLY BEATEN

3 TBSP MINCED FRESH PARSLEY

1 TBSP SUGAR

3/4 CUP SLICED ALMONDS, TOASTED AND LIGHTLY CRUSHED WITH A ROLLING PIN

10 SHEETS PHYLLO DOUGH

3/4 CUP CLARIFIED BUTTER

CONFECTIONERS' SUGAR

Heat olive oil in a deep pan over medium heat. Add onions and cook until translucent, about 5 minutes. Add cinnamon stick, ginger, saffron, and salt and pepper to taste. Stir in ⅓ cup water, then place squabs breast side down in pan. Reduce heat to low and cook, covered, for 30 minutes, turning once.

Remove squabs from pan and set aside to cool. Simmer onion mixture, uncovered, until pan juices are reduced by half, about 10 minutes. When squabs are cool enough to handle, remove and discard skin and bones with your fingers, then finely shred meat. Place meat in a bowl, then stir in 1 tsp. cinnamon and 1 tsp. orange-flower water. Set squab mixture aside.

Whisk eggs into reduced pan juices, then mix in remaining 2 tsp. cinnamon, parsley, sugar, remaining 3 tsp. orange-flower water, and almonds. Cook until eggs have scrambled and absorbed all juices, so that consistency is somewhat dry, about 2 minutes. Remove from heat and set aside.

Place 1 sheet phyllo on a clean surface and brush with butter; place a second sheet over it and brush with butter. Place buttered sheets centered over an 8" plate. Repeat phyllo process three times, laying each pair of sheets at an angle over previous sheets to form an irregular bottom crust. Center squab mixture on crust and top with almond mixture. Prepare remaining 2 phyllo sheets as above and place atop almond mixture. Fold overhanging bottom sheets over to completely enclose filling. Brush top with clarified butter to seal.

Heat 2 tbsp. clarified butter over medium heat in a nonstick frying pan large enough to hold bestila. Carefully slide bestila into pan and fry until sides turn golden brown, about 3 minutes. Cover bestila with a large plate, then carefully flip it over onto plate. Add remaining 1 tbsp. butter to pan, slide bestila back into pan on uncooked side, and fry about another 2 minutes. Slide onto a serving dish, sprinkle all over with confectioners' sugar and serve.

Pomegranate Gelato
With espresso

1 CUP HEAVY CREAM

1 CUP WHOLE MILK

3/4 CUP SUGAR

1 1/2 TBSP CORNSTARCH

1/8 TSP FINE SEA SALT

1 1/4 CUPS BOTTLED POMEGRANATE JUICE

1/3 CUP CRÈME DE CASSIS, POMEGRANATE LIQUEUR, OR FRUIT DESSERT WINE

1 TSP FRESHLY SQUEEZED LEMON JUICE

In a medium pot, whisk together the cream, milk, sugar, cornstarch, and salt. Bring to a boil over medium-high heat, whisking occasionally. When the mixture boils, reduce the heat to maintain a lively simmer and cook, whisking constantly, for two minutes.

Scrape the mixture into a medium bowl and add the pomegranate juice, liqueur, or wine and lemon juice. Whisk to combine thoroughly.

Chill the mixture for at least an hour, either in the fridge or by carefully setting the bowl into a larger bowl of ice water and stirring occasionally.

Freeze in an ice cream maker according to the manufacturer's instructions. The gelato will be very soft (although perfectly edible!) at this point and will firm up if transferred to an airtight container and placed in the freezer for a few hours. Homemade gelato is always best eaten within a day or two, but this will keep in the freezer for a week or more.

Adapted from Gourmet Magazine (September 2006)

TULANE CONTRIBUTOR

Frank Weiner (TUSA 1980)

Professor Frank H. Weiner has educated, along with many superb colleagues, hundreds of architects since 1987. He has taught in the School of Architecture + Design at Virginia Tech over the past three decades and served in a variety of leadership positions including Head of the Department of Architecture and subsequently as the Founding Interim Director of the School of Architecture + Design (established in 2003). His scholarship is on the relationship between architecture, philosophy and education. It has been presented at conferences in the US and around the world. He has taught design studios, required courses, and seminars at both the undergraduate and graduate levels. He is the recipient of the 2003-2005 European Association of Architectural Educators prize for his essay entitled "Five Critical Horizons for Architectural Educators in an Age of Distraction". He was also a co-recipient of the 2016 Association of Collegiate Schools of Architecture Design-Build Award. Professor Weiner is the founding curator of the Lucy and Olivio Ferrari Archive at Virginia Tech established in 2017. He is a graduate of Tulane University (B. Arch. 1980), Columbia University (M.S. Building Design 1987), and is a registered architect.

FAVORITE RECIPE

Prosecco spumante extra dry served with favorite olives and hand broken chunks of Parmigiano-Reggiano stravecchio (extra-aged) cheese.

RIGHT: SAN CARLO ALLE QUATTRO FONTANE (ROME, ITALY) DESIGNED BY BORROMINI
PHOTO BY FRANK WEINER

Henri Labrouste

PARIS, FRANCE
1801 - 1875

Christopher Thomas

TUSA 1980

BIBLIOTHÈQUE ST GENEVIÈVE, EXTERIOR (PARIS, FRANCE) DESIGNED BY HENRI LABROUSTE

My dinner guest selection is **HENRI LABROUSTE**, architect in Paris of both the Bibliothèque Nationale de France and the Bibliothèque St. Geneviève.

Labrouste was born and lived his early life in Paris. His father, a public administrator, had been a member of the Directory during the Terror, and was nearly beheaded. He was saved through the intervention of relatives of Robespierre who was himself beheaded; so it seems his relatives must have cared more for Labrouste than for him. Labrouste's mother, Anne-Dominique Gourg, was daughter of a family of Cognac merchants.

Henri entered the École des Beaux-Arts in 1819, and in 1824 won the Grand Prix de Rome and studied Roman construction at the Medici Villa in Rome. On his return home, he opened a studio at the École des Beaux-Arts and was a major proponent of rationalist design.

In both libraries, Labrouste's work is an elegant wedding of the modern use of iron and the framework of restrained classicism in stone. As lugubrious as the reading room he designed for the Bibliothèque Nationale first appears, it is really an elegant solution to spanning a large open area with a comparatively lightweight structure; a series of iron and glass pendentive domes supported on straw-thin iron columns, appearing all the more slender next to the stone pilasters that surround the perimeter of the space. In the earlier Bibliothèque St Geneviève, Labrouste created a deceptively simple linear neoclassical building. Inside, Labrouste placed the reading room on the second floor over a stone pillared ground floor. The reading room is again spanned by a lightweight iron structure, only this time using a pair of continuous vaults supported by castellated iron arches. The structure is supported on both heavy stone perimeter walls and thin iron columns in the middle.

- Christopher Thomas (TUSA 1980)

BIBLIOTHÈQUE ST GENEVIÈVE, INTERIOR (PARIS, FRANCE) DESIGNED BY HENRI LABROUSTE

| Henri Labrouste | Dinner Party |

APPETIZER
Stuffed Cucumbers

DRINK
Sidecar Cocktail

MAIN COURSE
Shrimp Flambé à la Henri Labrouste

IN ORDER TO IMAGINE what Labrouste may have served when he gave a dinner party, I consulted a copy of the most famous French cookbook of his time. In 1869, Alexandre Dumas, author of *The Count of Monte Cristo* and many other wonderful stories, finished what he considered to be one of his greatest works, Grand Dictionnaire de Cuisine. In over 600 pages, Dumas chronicled (in alphabetical order) recipes, ingredients, and techniques. More than a dictionary, though, it is a work of literature in the way he weaves it together as a story and enlivens it with many anecdotes. Many of the recipes in it are nearly identical or incipient versions of what you would find in a cookbook today, though with more trans fats. A moment's perusal easily turns up something Henri Labrouste surely served at a dinner party at some time.

Since Labrouste came from Bordeaux with family in the cognac business, I chose items to serve which feature cognac as a major ingredient, but also have a New Orleans accent so he would know I was from Tulane! The first is my own Shrimp Flambé à la Henri Labrouste; The second is a Sidecar Cocktail. The parent of the Sidecar is the Brandy Crusta, a cocktail that has its roots in New Orleans. Shrimp, cognac, fire. What could go wrong?

- *Christopher Thomas*

Stuffed Cucumbers

Peel and trim 3 or 4 cucumbers. Cut off the stem end. With a larding needle, remove all the seeds [note, thankfully today we have seedless cucumbers…]. Rinse well in water with a dash of vinegar. Blanch in boiling water. Dip in cold water. Drain. Stuff with chopped white chicken meat, bread, herbs, spices, and whole eggs to bind. Line the bottom with bacon and put your cucumbers on it. Season with salt, pepper, a bouquet of parsley, scallions, and 2 cloves. Add 1 tablespoon of rich broth. Cover with paper and bring to a boil. Simmer. Drain. Sauce with a sharpened, reduced espagnole.

SAUCE ESPAGNOLE, STUFFED CUCUMBERS, SIDECAR
ILLUSTRATION BY CHRISTOPHER THOMAS

SECTION THROUGH FLAMBÉ

SHRIMP FLAMBÉ À LA HENRI LABROUSTE
ILLUSTRATIONS BY CHRISTOPHER THOMAS

Shrimp Flambé à la Henri Labrouste

1 LB MEDIUM SHRIMP, PEELED
AND DEVEINED

4 TBSP BUTTER

1/4 CUP COGNAC

1/4 CUP DRY VERMOUTH

1 CUP DICED ROMA TOMATOES

1 MEDIUM SHALLOT, FINELY CHOPPED

1/4 CUP FLAT LEAF PARSLEY

1/2 TSP DRIED BASIL

1/2 TSP DRIED OREGANO

1/2 TSP SWEET PAPRIKA

1/4 TSP CAYENNE OR TO TASTE

Never flambé without an audience. It's way too much work without someone there to watch, and it is essential to have someone nearby to dial 911 should the necessity arise.

Heat the pan over medium high heat. Add butter till it melts and sizzles. Add shrimp. Cook until shrimp have turned pink. Take pan off heat, pour in cognac. Tilt pan away from you (see section) and put back over flame (this assumes you are cooking with gas). Should ignite cognac immediately. If on electric, you're on your own.

Alcohol should burn off in about 30 seconds. Add vermouth, tomatoes, shallot, and spices. Lower heat to medium. Cook for three more minutes and serve on plates with a mound of white rice in the middle, and sprinkle with parsley.

Sidecar Cocktail

1.5 OZ COGNAC

3-4 OZ COINTREAU

3-4 OZ FRESH LEMON JUICE

GARNISH: LEMON WEDGE

For each serving, put in a shaker filled with ice.

Shake vigorously and pour. Use your best judgement whether to do this before or after Flambéing.

TULANE CONTRIBUTOR

Christopher Thomas (TUSA 1980)

I am an architect practicing in Illinois, a castaway in a strange land. I am way too far from the cuisine of New Orleans that I was fortunate enough to experience daily for a decade. Fortunately, the architecture and food of New Orleans accompany me wherever I go. When I am not practicing architecture, I am either cooking for my family, playing music with a community wind ensemble, or working in my wood shop.

PLAZA (CHRISTOPHER THOMAS)

MIXED-USE DEVELOPMENT (CHRISTOPHER THOMAS)

BIBLIOTHÈQUE ST. GENEVIÈVE   ILLUSTRATION BY CHRISTOPHER THOMAS

NOTABLE ARCHITECT

Henry Hobson Richardson

ST. JAMES PARISH, LOUISIANA
1838 - 1886

TULANE CONTRIBUTOR

Desmond Brown

TULANE UNIVERSITY 1980

NEW YORK STATE CAPITOL BUILDING (ALBANY, NY) DESIGNED BY HENRY HOBSON RICHARDSON

HENRY HOBSON RICHARDSON

was born at his grandfather's sugarcane plantation upriver from New Orleans. He briefly attended the University of Louisiana (later Tulane University) before enrolling at Harvard, where he graduated in 1858. He spent the next six years in Paris, studying at the École des Beaux-Arts. Richardson's life and work bridged North and South, the old world and the new, antebellum times and the Gilded Age. He traveled widely but never returned to Louisiana.

In 1872, he won the competition to build Trinity Church in Boston, and in 1874 he moved with his wife and four children to Brookline, Massachusetts. During the next dozen years, Richardson "towered like a monadnock over the architectural world." (O'Gorman, Living Architecture: A Biography of H.H. Richardson, p. 159.) His Brookline office produced a steady stream of civic buildings, stately homes, and libraries. Richardson's gregarious, oversized personality was matched by his appetite for fine food, wine, and spirits, enjoyed with colleagues and clients. Augustus Saint-Gaudens shared a dinner with Richardson at which he drank nearly a magnum of champagne accompanied by "enormous quantities of cheese." (O'Gorman, p. 116) His client Frances Glessner said he was the largest man she had ever seen. He died in 1886 at age 47.

I appreciate the elegant polychrome splendor of his churches and libraries, the organic beauty of his shingled homes, his dedication to craft. If we had shared a meal, we would have celebrated North and South, ancient and modern, and wished a longer life for us both.

- *Desmond Brown (Tulane University 1980)*

AUSTIN HALL (CAMBRIDGE, MA) DESIGNED BY HENRY HOBSON RICHARDSON

Henry Hobson Richardson	Dinner Party

APPETIZER
Mirlitons* Stuffed with Shrimp

DRINK
Automne en Normandie

MAIN COURSE
Audrey's New England Fish Chowder

Audrey's New England Fish Chowder

1-2 LBS HADDOCK (COD, SCROD, OR COMBINATION)

1 ONION DICED

2 TBSP OLIVE OIL

1 TBSP BUTTER

1 BOTTLE OF CLAM JUICE

2 CUPS MILK

2 CUPS HALF AND HALF

SALT AND PEPPER TO TASTE

3 - 4 MEDIUM POTATOES (E.G. YUKON GOLD), PEELED AND CUBED

MIX OF THYME, MARJORAM, SAGE, AND FENNEL SEED; USE 1 TSP OR TO TASTE.

In saucepan, add olive oil, butter, and diced onion. Cook on low or medium heat until soft.

Add cubed potatoes and ¼ cup water and cook for about 10 minutes, until tender.

Place fish in saucepan with ingredients, cover and cook for about 20 minutes or until fish falls into large pieces.

When fish is cooked, add half and half, milk, and clam juice. Add the herb mix, 1 tsp or to taste. Do not boil.

Serve with fresh chopped parsley and a dab of butter on top.

Mirlitons are a fall staple in New Orleans, sometimes grown on backyard vines and stuffed with cheese, bread, or shrimp. They have a delicate, wholesome flavor that pairs well with other more adventurous and spicy dishes.

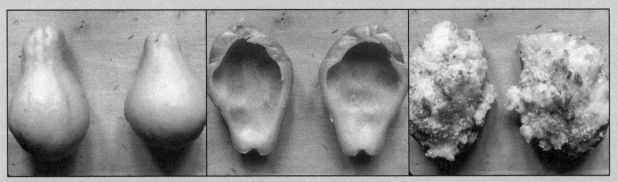

Mirlitons Stuffed with Shrimp

3 MIRLITONS (CHAYOTES)

3/4 POUND RAW SHRIMP

4 TBSP BUTTER

1 CUP FINELY CHOPPED ONION

1 TSP MINCED GARLIC

2 TBSP FLOUR

1 CUP MILK

1/4 CUP FINELY CHOPPED
GREEN ONIONS

1 EGG YOLK

1/2 CUP FRESH BREAD CRUMBS

1/2 CUP GRATED CHEDDAR CHEESE

Cut the mirlitons in half lengthwise, place in a pot of cold water, add salt, and bring to a boil. Simmer only about ten minutes, no longer, or the mirlitons will become too soft. Drain and run under cold water.

Using a sharp teaspoon or melon-baller, scoop out the flesh and seeds of each half and save. Leave the shells about 1/4 inch to 1/8 inch thick. Chop the flesh and seeds and save; there should be about 1 cup. Peel and de-vein the shrimp, then chop coarsely and set aside. Preheat oven to 425 degrees.

Heat 2 tablespoons butter in a saucepan or Dutch oven and add the onion and garlic. Cook until the onions are translucent, then sprinkle with the flour and stir to distribute evenly. Add the milk, stirring with a whisk.

When the sauce is thickened, add the chopped pulp. Bring to a boil while stirring, and add in the scallions. Remove the mixture from the heat, and stir in the egg yolk. Let stand to room temperature. Stir in the shrimp, salt, pepper, and bread crumbs.

Stuff the mirliton halves with the mixture. Mix the remaining bread crumbs with the cheese and distribute it over the stuffing, generously. Bake 20 minutes on lightly buttered baking dish.

Automne en Normandie

1 APPLE

2 OZ CALVADOS

1/2 OZ FRESH LEMON JUICE

1/2 OZ HONEY SYRUP
(HONEY DILUTED WITH EQUAL
AMOUNT HOT WATER.)

In the bottom of a cocktail shaker, muddle 1/4 of a crisp, tart apple. Add ice along with the Calvados, lemon juice and honey syrup. Shake, then strain through a fine mesh strainer into a glass with fresh ice. Garnish with an apple slice and ground cinnamon.

Desmond Brown (Tulane University 1980)

Desmond Brown grew up in a house designed by a Tulane architect, and counts several graduates of the Tulane School of Architecture as lifelong friends. He has no talent for design or drawing, or for cooking to be honest, but admires those who do.

He practices orthopaedic surgery instead, mostly in Boston and sometimes in Cambodia, which he considers his second home. His architectural interests include twentieth-century modernist churches, and institutions for the treatment of mental illness.

Pistachio Ice Cream

Simply the best ice cream flavor there is. Time-consuming to make, but so many good things are. Use fresh, unsalted pistachios. The custard base made from the egg yolks creates a smoother, richer mix. Avoid food coloring and you will get a beautiful olive/ochre color. I use a Cuisinart two-quart home ice-cream maker.

3 CUPS UNSALTED SHELLED PISTACHIO NUTS

1.5 CUPS SUGAR

2 CUPS WHOLE MILK

2 CUPS LIGHT CREAM

DASH OF SALT

7 EGG YOLKS

1/2 TSP ALMOND EXTRACT

MAKES ABOUT TWO QUARTS

Combine the pistachios with 1/4 cup sugar in a blender or food processor. Pulse until finely chopped. In a heavy saucepan, add the chopped pistachios to the milk and cream, and bring to a simmer at medium heat. Remove from the heat, cover, and let steep at room temperature for thirty minutes to allow the pistachio flavor to develop. Stir in the remaining sugar and heat until the sugar dissolves.

Beat the egg yolks lightly in a medium bowl, and gradually whisk in a cup of the warm pistachio milk. Whisk the egg mixture into the remaining pistachio milk in the saucepan, and reduce the heat, stirring until the custard thickens enough to coat the back of a spoon, no more than 170-175 degrees F. Use a thermometer to monitor the temperature; the eggs will solidify if heated too much. Strain the custard into a bowl, and discard the nuts. Refrigerate for 4 hours or until the custard is very cold.

Pour the custard into the ice cream maker and run it until it becomes hard to scrape from the canister. Pack into cartons and freeze an additional few hours or overnight.

53616 TRINITY CHURCH, BOSTON.

Charles Follen McKim

CHESTER COUNTY, PA
1847 - 1909

Bill Barry

TUSA 1980

BOSTON PUBLIC LIBRARY, MCKIM BUILDING

The trio of MCKIM, MEAD, & WHITE is a firm well-known in architectural history for notable classical design. Charles McKim designed the Boston Public Library at Copley Square, completed 1895, where I spent a significant part of my career learning to balance creativity with respect when practicing in the context of such remarkable history. McKim's library is a beautifully proportioned and impeccably detailed icon that we all remember from architectural history class, but it was also a decorated masonry pile in need of care and contemporary development.

Master of classical design, dedicated educator, and a leader of his profession, McKim was a giant of architectural history. He was also a generous collaborator of soft-spoken self-confidence, and a loyal friend and benefactor to numerous colleagues. In pursuit of his ideals of proportion, fitness, and beauty, he was quiet, modest, respectful, but relentless. McKim saw design as a collaborative act, and drew from the skills of an array of artists, staff, and partners. Today, we value buildings of his for their craft and materiality. He knew that success was dependent on skilled execution – not unlike a good recipe, which is architecture of a different sort.

McKim's library design took inspiration from the Bibliothèque Sainte-Geneviève in Paris by Henri Labrouste (featured by Christopher Thomas on page 32). It was modeled after a Renaissance palazzo, so his ornamented classical interiors focused on the piano nobile, leaving a creative opportunity on the ground floor for an aesthetic counterpoint. There he fully displayed overhead the simple yet elegant structural vaults of Rafael Guastavino's flat terra cotta tile system that was new to the United States. So for a recipe, I'm thinking classical with a twist.

- Bill Barry (TUSA 1980)

IMAGE COURTESY OF BILL BARRY

| Charles Follen McKim | Dinner Party |

MAIN COURSE
Chesapeake Oyster Stew

DRINK
New Orleans Milk Punch

New Orleans Milk Punch

2 OZ BOURBON OR BRANDY

1 TSP POWDERED SUGAR

1 SCOOP OF VANILLA ICE CREAM

1 OZ (FAT-FREE) HALF & HALF CREAM
PLUS 2 OZ FAT FREE REGULAR MILK

SEVERAL ICE CUBES

1 CAP FULL VANILLA EXTRACT

1 CAP FULL AMARETTO EXTRACT

Blend in mixer on "medium" setting. Pour into double "old fashioned" glass. Dust with cinnamon (not nutmeg). Serve with love!

(Fat Free) Half & Half Cream PLUS 2 OZS. FAT FREE
(or regular milk) REG. MILK

Some Vanilla Extract (cap full)
SOME AMARETTO (TEASPOON FULL)
Blend in mixer on "Medium" setting

Chesapeake Oyster Stew

From Dylan Salmon of Dylan's Oyster Cellar, Baltimore, MD, focused on nostalgic Eastern Shore traditions. This is a simple blend of cream, celery, and oysters that makes up a classic "tried-and-true" oyster stew. Chopping the celery and shallots fine and using good-quality butter is key. Once the vegetables are softened, milk and cream are added along with just enough Tabasco and Worcestershire sauce to give the stew a touch of character. It's a very simple thing, but success is in the timing and temperature. The recipe anticipates New England Wellfleet or Rhode Island Salt Pond oysters, which are of higher salinity, so be prepared to adjust for your local variations.

1/4 CUP BUTTER, PLUS 2 TBSP. MELTED

1/2 CUP MINCED CELERY

1/3 CUP MINCED SHALLOT

ABOUT 1 CUP LIQUOR FROM FRESHLY SHUCKED OYSTERS OR BOTTLED CLAM JUICE

3 CUPS WHOLE MILK

3 CUPS HEAVY CREAM

1/4 TSP WORCESTERSHIRE SAUCE

1/4 TSP TABASCO SAUCE

1/4 TSP SALT

ABOUT 30 OYSTERS, FRESHLY SHUCKED. (OR 1 TO 2 PINTS OF PRE-SHUCKED OYSTERS, DEPENDING ON SIZE.)

1/2 CUP FINELY CHOPPED CURLY PARSLEY

FRESHLY GROUND BLACK PEPPER

Melt 1/4 cup butter in a saucepan over medium heat. Add celery and shallot and sauté until just soft, about 3 minutes. Add oyster liquor or clam juice, milk, and cream, and bring the mixture to a gentle simmer. Stir in Worcestershire sauce, Tabasco, and salt. Add the oysters to the base and poach for about two minutes. Remove with a slotted spoon, dividing the oysters between warmed serving bowls.

Taste the base and adjust for more Worcestershire, Tabasco, or salt, if needed. Bring to a boil over high heat and immediately ladle the soup over the oysters. Add 1 tsp. melted butter, a sprinkle of fresh parsley, and a generous grind of pepper to each bowl. Serve with oyster crackers.

From Dylan Salmon of Dylan's Oyster Cellar (Baltimore, MD)

Bill Barry (TUSA 1980)

After Tulane, I was only in architectural practice for a few years when the World's Fair came to New Orleans in 1984. It was like joining the circus. That valuable experience fueled my curiosity and I moved to Boston, where my timing was good, and I enjoyed over twenty years of fascinating architectural practice on landmark buildings, many of them libraries. That was followed by a number of interesting years in the administration of an historic non-profit. Based on those diverse experiences as both architect and owner, I now focus on early strategic thinking and creative planning to set clients up for success in the revitalization and restoration of their historic structures.

I learned a lot from Charles McKim and his collaborative nature. The collaboration required for the library's restoration and revitalization was extrordinary, and success was still dependent on the execution.

A native of New Orleans, I offer two hometown favorites, and I like that they are both about the execution. First is the Sazerac cocktail. The ingredients are simple, but the proportions and process are key. The good news is that the only way to get it right is with practice. Then, skip right to dessert with Banana's Foster. It has ice cream for Mr. McKim, and requires practice as well, because you're putting on a show. My dad loved to make it for us.

FAVORITE RECIPE

Bananas Foster

4 BANANAS	1/2 TSP CINNAMON
1/4 POUND BUTTER	1/4 CUP BANANA LIQUEUR
1 CUP BROWN SUGAR	1/4 CUP DARK RUM

New Orleans, as a major port city, has always enjoyed fresh bananas shipped in from Latin America. Chef Paul Blange was asked by Owen Brennan of Brennan's Restaurant to create a recipe using this fruit. In 1951, Chef Paul created Bananas Foster naming it for Owen's good friend and fellow member of the New Orleans Crime Commission, Richard Foster. Today, almost 20 tons of bananas are flamed each year at Brennan's in the preparation of this now world-famous dessert.

Cut bananas in half lengthwise then dice into 1-inch cubes. In a heavy bottom sauté pan, melt butter over medium-high heat. Add sugar and cinnamon and whisk until bubbly and sugar is melted. Stir in banana liqueur and diced bananas and sauté until softened. Remove the pan from the flame. Add rum then return pot to heat, taking care, as rum will ignite. Stir constantly and when flames subside, remove from heat and serve as a topping over vanilla ice cream or your favorite cheesecake.

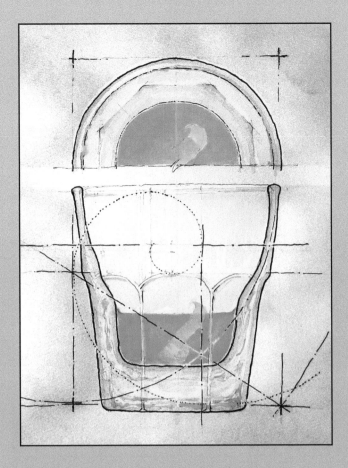

ILLUSTRATION BY BILL BARRY

Sazerac

The epitome of simple elegance, dependent on proportion and execution. Plenty of opportunity for variations to personal taste. Originally made in the 19th century with cognac, the period of significance we are focused on is the 20th century classic made with rye whiskey.

Chill in advance a Rocks or Old Fashioned glass. The thicker glass holds the chill so the drink can be served neat. In a separate mixing glass, combine simple syrup, bitters and whiskey. Add ice and stir vigorously, don't shake, just long enough to be well chilled. Coat the inside of the chilled serving glass with absinthe, pouring out any excess. Strain the mixture into the serving glass neat. Twist the lemon peel, wipe the rim, and either add as garnish or discard.

2OZ RYE WHISKEY (YOUR FAVORITE – LOTS OUT THERE THESE DAYS)

3 - 4 DASHES OF PEYCHAUD'S BITTERS

1/4 OZ SIMPLE SYRUP
(OR 1 TSP SUGAR + 1 TSP WATER)

1/4 OZ ABSINTHE
(OR SIMILAR PASTIS OF YOUR CHOICE)

LEMON PEEL

Antoni Gaudí

REUS, SPAIN
1852 - 1926

Doug Wittnebel

TUSA 1980

LA SAGRADA FAMILIA (BARCELONA, SPAIN) DESIGNED BY ANTONI GAUDÍ

ANTONI GAUDÍ was a Catalan architect recognized as one of the most creative experts in the art of Architecture. He was born on the 25th of June 1852 and as a child, Gaudí's health was delicate, so he spent long periods of time at the summer house in Riudoms studying the surrounding nature. His family were boilermakers, which most likely allowed the young designer to develop a skill for working with three-dimensional space and volume as he helped his father and grandfather in the family workshop. His talent for designing spaces and understanding materials resulted in a collection of unique, personal spaces and buildings composed in an architectural language that continues to seduce every new generation of designers.

I experienced the real Gaudí creations in the Summer of 1979, and remember the incredible feelings that his buildings could stimulate, and wish I still had some of those drawings and sketches from that trip to Barcelona.

- *Doug Wittnebel (TUSA 1980)*

PARC GUELL (BARCELONA, SPAIN) DESIGNED BY ANTONI GAUDÍ

Antoni Gaudí	Dinner Party

Gumbo

Classic Mojito

Twirled Tower of Creamy Frozen Yogurt*

*Purchase Frozen Yogurt from your favorite ice cream shop

Gumbo

1/2 CUP FLOUR

4 TBSP BUTTER

1 GREEN OR RED BELL PEPPER, CHOPPED

2-3 CELERY STALKS, CHOPPED

3 CLOVES GARLIC

1 LB DICED TOMATOES

7 OR MORE OKRA, DICED

4 CUPS CHICKEN BROTH

1 LB SHRIMP, PEELED AND DE-VEINED

1 LB ANDOUILLE SAUSAGE, SLICED

1 TBSP OREGANO

1 TBSP THYME

1 TBSP CAJUN SPICE

SALT AND PEPPER

Gather all ingredients. First, the Roux: Melt butter over medium-low heat, then add flour. Cook, stirring constantly, until a dark caramel color.

Add onions, pepper, and celery and stir until soft. Then, add garlic, sausage, and cajun seasoning.

Add tomatoes, chicken broth, and okra. Bring to a boil, then reduce heat and simmer, stirring every 5 minutes. Scrape the sides when needed.

After 1 hour, add the shrimp and cook until pink. Serve on top of a white rice pyramid. Enjoy!

ILLUSTRATIONS BY DOUG WITTNEBEL

Trencadís
also known as pique assiette
using broken ceramic tile = mosaic

ANTONI GAUDÍ

COFFEE FLAVOR

TWIRLED TOWER OF CREAMY FROZEN YOGURT

WITH SPRINKLES

DESSERT

GUMBO

TULANE CONTRIBUTOR

Doug Wittnebel (TUSA 1980)

Doug Wittnebel is an architect, designer, illustrator, and artist based in California. He combines a unique viewpoint, a knowledge of cool aesthetics, a sense of humor, an undying interest in visual phenomena, a deep sense of history, combined with multiple layers of very sound practical experiences as a free hand drawer and designer. He has been seasoned with 13 years of work and travel in Asia plus 20 years of Cali sunshine in addition to a childhood raised in New Orleans.

Doug is also known as the Designer that cannot stop drawing. Drawing is a basis for many creative acts. He is also known for teaching young students about the magic of sketching and drawing.

"The more you draw, the more you can decipher the hidden depths of the creative process," he says. "The process of group and individual sketching becomes the spark for igniting new possibilities."

FAVORITE RECIPE

Classic Mojito

10 OR 11 FRESH MINT LEAVES

1/2 LIME, CUT INTO 4 WEDGES

2 TABLESPOONS WHITE SUGAR,
OR TO TASTE

1 CUP ICE CUBES

1 1/2 FLUID OUNCES WHITE RUM

1/2 CUP CLUB SODA

Place the mint leaves and 1 lime wedge into a tall glass. Use a muddler to crush the mint and lime to release the mint oils and lime juice. Add 2 more lime wedges and the white sugar, and muddle again to release the lime juice. Do not strain the mixture.

Fill the glass almost to the top with ice. Pour the rum over the ice, and fill the glass with club soda. Stir, taste, and add more sugar if desired. Garnish with the remaining lime wedge.

Henry Stuart

NAMPA, IDAHO
1856 - 1947

Mac Walcott

TUSA 1980

HENRY STUART COTTAGE (ABOVE: EXTERIOR, RIGHT: INTERIOR) (PHOTOS COURTESY OF MAC WALCOTT)

Henry Stuart | Traditional Meal

Henry James Stuart (writing in the Birmingham Age Herald newspaper, March 3, 1929):

Something of the simple life might be illustrated in my preparation and use of simple food. Almost invariably for years I have had a breakfast of fresh mush made of nearly equal parts choice corn and wheat ground in my own hand mill each day as I need it. It is made in the morning as soon as breakfast is over and steamed for two or three hours at least, then put away until the next morning. Not more than a teaspoon of corn oil is used in the frying pan and it is browned to a turn on one side. Some very sweet tea is poured over the mush and it is eaten as soon as cool enough. The remaining tea is sipped with bread or toast and completes my breakfast, which is simple and costs less than three cents! On this I can work all day if necessary.

Dinner [what Southerners used to call lunch] usually consists of some vegetable—dasheens or sweet potatoes—which I grow myself. Some bread or toast is eaten with a little honey. Cost, less than five cents.

Supper for quite a while has been sweetened clabber and bread. Some graham crackers are eaten, too, and these are my nearest approach to pastry. Cost of a frugal supper, within five cents.

I have plenty of canned sand pears, and often have these with bread or toast make a supper. Day-old bread is bought in Fairhope at six cents per loaf instead of ten cents. If I fail to get this, I bake my own bread from my own meal. By keeping a good supply of toast made when the bread is abundant, I seldom have to bake. Graham bread is usually to be obtained, and if not rye, so I seldom buy white bread.

The high cost of living does not worry me at all—nor am I ever sick. Appetite is sharp and keen when [breakfast] mealtime comes, but I can postpone indefinitely dinner or supper. Thoreau's friends accused him of living upon buttermilk and greens, but I have not quite reached this point. My simple life proves right through my ability to do what, to many, are none other than wonders.

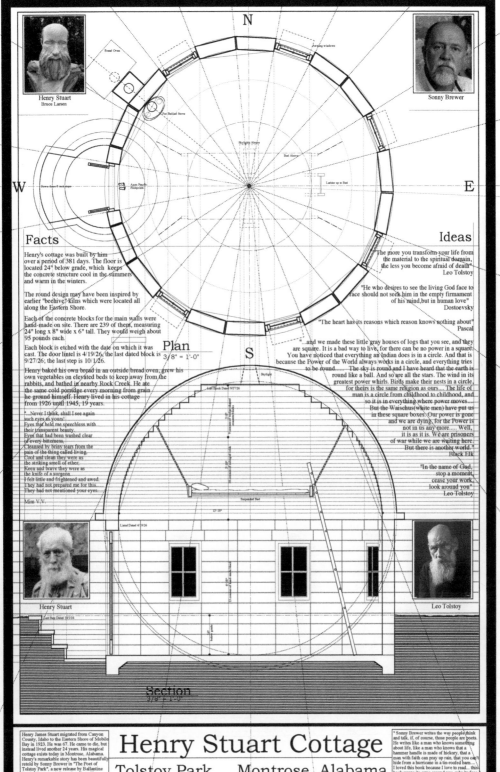

N

Henry Stuart
Bruce Larsen

Sonny Brewer

W

E

Facts

Henry's cottage was built by him over a period of 381 days. The floor is located 24" below grade, which keeps the concrete structure cool in the summers and warm in the winters.

The round design may have been inspired by earlier "beehive" kilns which were located all along the Eastern Shore.

Each of the concrete blocks for the main walls were hand-made on site. There are 239 of them, measuring 24" long x 8" wide x 6" tall. They would weigh about 95 pounds each.

Each block is etched with the date on which it was cast. The door lintel is 4/19/26; the last dated block is 9/27/26; the last step is 10/1/26.

Henry baked his own bread in an outside bread oven, grew his own vegetables on elevated beds to keep away from the rabbits, and bathed in nearby Rock Creek. He ate the same cold porridge every morning from grain he ground himself. Henry lived in his cottage from 1926 until 1945, 19 years.

"...Never I think, shall I see again
such eyes as yours!
Eyes that held me speechless with
their transparent beauty.
Eyes that had been washed clear
of every bitterness,
Cleansed by briny tears from the
pain of the thing called living,
Cool and clean they were as
the striking smell of ether;
Keen and brave they were as
the knife of a surgeon
I felt little and frightened and awed.
They had not prepared me for this...
They had not mentioned your eyes."
Miss V.V.

Plan
3/8" = 1'-0"

S

Ideas

"The more you transform your life from the material to the spiritual domain, the less you become afraid of death"
Leo Tolstoy

"He who desires to see the living God face to face should not seek him in the empty firmament of his mind, but in human love"
Dostoevsky

"The heart has its reasons which reason knows nothing about"
Pascal

"...and we made these little gray houses of logs that you see, and they are square. It is a bad way to live, for there can be no power in a square. You have noticed that everything an Indian does is in a circle. And that is because the Power of the World always works in a circle, and everything tries to be round...... The sky is round and I have heard that the earth is round like a ball. And so are all the stars. The wind in its greatest power whirls. Birds make their nests in a circle, for theirs is the same religion as ours... The life of man is a circle from childhood to childhood, and so it is in everything where power moves... But the Waischus(white men) have put us in these square boxes. Our power is gone and we are dying, for the Power is not in us any more..... Well, it is as it is. We are prisoners of war while we are waiting here. But there is another world."
Black Elk

"In the name of God, stop a moment, cease your work, look around you"
Leo Tolstoy

Henry Stuart

Leo Tolstoy

Section
3/8" = 1'-0"

Henry James Stuart migrated from Canyon County, Idaho to the Eastern Shore of Mobile Bay in 1923. He was 67. He came to die, but instead lived another 24 years. His magical cottage exists today in Montrose, Alabama. Henry's remarkable story has been beautifully retold by Sonny Brewer in "The Poet of Tolstoy Park", a new release by Ballantine Books. For more information about Henry Stuart and Sonny Brewer, go to his website. Over the Transom Books .com

Henry Stuart Cottage
Tolstoy Park   Montrose, Alabama

" Sonny Brewer writes the way people think and talk, if, of course, those people are poets. He writes like a man who knows something about life, like a man who knows that a hammer handle is made of hickory, that a man with faith can pray up rain, that you can't hide from a hurricane in a tin-roofed barn... I loved this book because I love to read... this book wraps its arms around you, rubs its face against yours with a stubbled cheek, and refuses to let you go."
RICK BRAGG

Love, memory, architecture

All that Henry's life did, all that those circular blocks do, all that Sonny's book will do, is allow us to remember; allow us to dream about another time like ours when Moderns like Henry (like us) tried to remember a timeless way of living, a boundless way of loving one another. And this memory of love is a wonderful thing; it is most of what we need. If stones and words placed carefully together can become the seeds of memory and then love, our years have not been wasted. Stones and words placed without love are vanity. (We are all so vain.)

C.M. Walcott 2/01/05; for PCWA, for Sonny, for the love of books. Thanks to Ken Niemeyer for saving it.

Bernard
Maybeck

NEW YORK, NEW YORK
1862 - 1957

Martin Bailkey

TUSA 1982

FIRST CHURCH OF CHRIST, SCIENTIST (BERKELEY, CALIFORNIA) DESIGNED BY BERNARD MAYBECK

As a free-range adolescent summering in the East Bay, stumbling upon the work of **BERNARD RALPH MAYBECK** was my first inkling that great architecture is an art, emerges from deep within the artist, and cannot be taught. The specific vehicle for the inkling was the First Church of Christ, Scientist (1910) in Berkeley. Its street presence was striking and alluring, the doors were unlocked, and I made my way in, not sure what to expect. What I discovered stays in my memory as among the finest displays of how materials, with their individual character and presence, are, through knowledge, craft and intuition, combined into a spiritual and life-affirming space.

The sensitivity to and crafting of traditional and modern materials seen in the Christian Science Church was also consistent throughout Maybeck's residential designs. The idea of "home" was strongly conveyed in shared spaces – living and dining rooms – distinguished by their joinery, and in landscaping that knitted the buildings to their hillside sites. But Maybeck also excelled at creating memorable spaces of passage – entry halls, foyers, and, in particular, wood-paneled stairways and landings that might include a simple bench as a place of rest.

A 1923 article in *Sunset* allowed Maybeck to introduce his ideas for modest houses that separated service spaces from a large single room partitioned for living, dining and sleeping. The first of these to be built was the Staniford house (1925) in the Oakland hills. Later altered, the house was destroyed in the October 1991 Oakland-Berkeley fire. In its original form, it's the Maybeck house I can best imagine growing older and wiser in; a home that fosters the contemplation of Nature, Dwelling, and Being over simple meals of soup, bread and wine.

- *Martin Bailkey (TUSA 1982)*

Warren P. Staniford house, 6130 Ocean View Drive, Oakland, 1925.
Documents Collection, C.E.D.

Although not technically one room, the Staniford house was basically contained in one area and formed a pleasant utilitarian space.

217

INTERIOR OF THE STANIFORD HOUSE (OAKLAND, CA 1925) (IMAGE COURTESY OF "BERNARD MAYBECK: ARTISAN, ARCHITECT, ARTIST" BY KENNETH H. CARDWELL, 1977)

| Bernard Maybeck | Dinner Party |

APPETIZER
Simple French Salad

DRINK
The Hemingway Daiquiri

MAIN COURSE
Traditional Bahamian Stew Fish

Maybeck's building materials, and how he partnered one material with another, are always clear and visually distinct – much like the materials in a simple salad! Maybeck was trained at the École des Beaux-Arts in Paris. He was influenced by his time in France, and I imagine he often thought back to those days. After returning to the US he worked in the New York office of Carrere & Hastings during the design and construction of the opulent Hotel Ponce de Leon (1888) in St. Augustine, Florida. Although the extent of his involvement in the hotel is not known, it possibly involved a site visit or two. I suspect his memories of Florida, like those of France, never left him – and see them manifested in his food and drink choices for imagined French/Floridian dinners shared with members of the Hillside Club, the group of Berkeley design influencers he belonged to (if the Hillside Club held potluck dinners).

- *Martin Bailkey*

Simple French Salad

1 HEAD, GREEN BOSTON LETTUCE

2 DICED SCALLIONS

1 TBSP DIJON MUSTARD

1 TSP LEMON JUICE

2-3 TBSP EXTRA VIRGIN OLIVE OIL

PEPPER AND SALT (TO TASTE, MORE PEPPER THAN SALT)

Carefully cut the lettuce's outer leaves on either side of the rib, then work around to the heart, cutting through the ribs lengthwise. Combine the lemon juice and mustard in a bowl, and add a little salt and pepper. Mix well, and add the olive oil. After more mixing, taste to see if more pepper and salt are desired.

Add the dressing to the lettuce and scallions just before serving.

Traditional Bahamian Stew Fish

2-3 POUNDS OF CLEANED AND SEASONED FISH, GROUPER OR SNAPPER PREFERRED

1/3 CUP COOKING OIL

3/4 CUP FLOUR

1 ONION, CHOPPED

1 MEDIUM-SIZED CHOPPED CARROT

1 MEDIUM-SIZED PEELED AND CHOPPED POTATO

3 TABLESPOONS TOMATO PASTE

THYME OR ANOTHER PREFERRED SPICE

Partially fry the fish until each side is brown. Heat the cooking oil in a heavy skillet, stirring in the flour until brown and not burnt. Add the browned fish, followed by the onion, carrot, potato, tomato paste and spice.

Place the blend in a pot having 6 cups of boiling water. Reduce heat and simmer for 15-20 minutes, making sure the fish is tender and well cooked. Serve, adding salt and pepper to taste.

Imagining Maybeck indulging his Florida memories through drink might, understandably, include a daiquiri. The daiquiri, however, was not introduced to Florida from Cuba until the early 20th century, after Maybeck's move West. So I'll take a bit of license and envision Maybeck as fond of both Florida and Hemingway.

The Hemingway Daiquiri

2 OUNCES WHITE RUM (TOP-SHELF IF YOU HAVE IT)

1/2 OZ MARASCHINO LIQUEUR

1/2 OZ FRESH GRAPEFRUIT JUICE

3/4 OZ FRESH LIME JUICE

1/4 OZ SIMPLE SYRUP (OPTIONAL)

A LIME WHEEL AS GARNISH

Pour the rum, maraschino liqueur, and grapefruit and lime juices (and simple syrup if desired) into an ice-filled cocktail shaker. Shake well, and strain into a chilled cocktail glass. Garnish with the lime wheel and serve.

THE PALACE OF FINE ARTS, SAN FRANCISCO DESIGNED BY BERNARD MAYBECK

Martin Bailkey (TUSA 1982)

During my Third Year at TUSA I realized that an architectural career was likely not in my future. But seeing great value in staying, I kept with it, graduated, and began a life of professional restlessness. Over the next 30 years I ventured through architecture, landscape architecture, and urban planning in various professional guises. Landscape architecture stuck the tightest, and I spent a good many years teaching it (along with some architecture and planning) at the university level in Oregon, Missouri, and Wisconsin.

In 1998, quite out of the blue, I was recruited into the nascent field of community food systems (manifested through farmers markets, community and school gardens, etc.). Over that time, I've been specifically engaged in urban agriculture, mostly with clean, unsoiled hands sitting in front of a computer screen. Through this work I've travelled extensively across the US, meeting truly inspiring and fascinating people. I've now landed as a project manager for Rooted, a food system organization in Madison, Wisconsin – where architecture, in the forms of F.L. Wright, is never far away.

Lentils and Rice

Several contributors to this collection revered New Orleans chef Paul Prudhomme, who passed away in 2015. His rise to prominence in the late 1970's coincided with our Tulane years, and K- Paul's Louisiana Kitchen, his Chartres Street restaurant, was a destination on return visits until its permanent closure in May 2020 as this book was being conceived. This is adapted from one of his recipes.

Begin by creating a seasoning mix in a bowl – 1 teaspoon each of salt, onion powder, garlic powder, dry mustard, dry sweet basil leaves, and dry thyme leaves; 2 teaspoons of sweet paprika; 1/2 teaspoon black pepper; 1/4 teaspoon cayenne.

The basic ingredients are simple and unfussy – 1 1/2 cups of dried lentils, 6 cups of chicken stock, 8 ounces of turkey or smoked ham, 1 1/2 cups of short-grain white rice – and chopped onions (2 1/2 cups), chopped green bell peppers (1/2 cup) and chopped celery (3/4 cup), the Holy Trinity of Louisiana cooking. Into a heavy, pre-heated (for 4-5 minutes) nonstick pot, add the bell peppers and one-half of the onions, and cook until browned. Add and stir the seasoning mix, lentils and meat for 2 minutes, then add the celery and rest of the onions and cook for 2 more minutes. Make sure to keep the pot bottom clear.

Stir in the chicken stock then add the rice. Bring everything to a boil, then reduce to low heat, cover and cook for 40 minutes or so until the lentils and rice are tender. Serve right away.

NOTABLE ARCHITECT

Guðjón
Samúelsson

ICELAND
1887 - 1950

TULANE CONTRIBUTOR

Jim Good

TUSA 1981

GUÐJÓN SAMÚELSSON is said to be the first Icelander to be formally educated in architecture. He was named the State Architect of Iceland in 1920, a year after graduating with a degree in architecture from the Royal Danish Academy of Fine Arts in Copenhagen. Over his thirty-year career, he shaped the look and feel of communities throughout the country with over 800 designs.

His portfolio includes public buildings, schools, lighthouses, and churches, arts centers, town plans, and private homes. Some of his most notable designs are the National Theatre of Iceland, the Landakot Roman Catholic Cathedral in Reykjavík, the Church at Akureyri, and his most recognized work - the Hallgrímskirkja - a Lutheran church in Reykjavík, commissioned in 1937.

The Hallgrímskirkja is a major landmark of Reykjavík, and its iconic profile completes the signature of the Reykjavík skyline, along with Guðjón's National Theatre building. Stark and dramatic, the Hallgrímskirkja is at once a Gothic revivalist effort in a country with no preexisting Gothic cathedrals, a product of the international Modernist and Art Deco movements, and a reflective statement on the nature of Iceland itself.

The church profile is said to be based on the natural geology of Iceland, namely the basalt columns at Svartifoss and Iceland's sharp mountain profiles, like the slim Hraundrangi peak in Öxnadalur.

- *Jim Good (TUSA 1981)*

LEFT AND ABOVE: HALLGRÍMSKIRKJA (REYKJAVÍK, ICELAND) DESIGNED BY SAMUELSSON

Guðjón Samúelsson	Dinner Party

MAIN COURSE
Grilled Halibut with
Lemon and Basil (with
a Side of Green Beans)

SIDE
Icelandic Rye Bread
with Butter

DRINK
Shots of Brinniven

DESSERT
No-Bake Skyr Cake

Eating in Iceland is direct and to the point – start with good food, then don't mess it up. The recipes above should be readily prepared, with things bought anyplace with a big market (you don't need to order anything from Reykjavík). You'll need to buy a few specific items, and then deal with them matter-of-factly and get them to the table fast.

This is a pretty quick dinner to make on a cold but clear fall day. If you are in the South and it just won't get cold, go for a raw, windy day in January or February. Use the grill outside for the halibut, without wearing a jacket, to expose yourself to as refreshing chilly an environment as you can arrange. Sipping shots of Brinniven as you grill the halibut will get you in the mood. There is also a bit of butter and cream in this, so maybe exercise first, and don't plan anything too demanding after the meal.

- Jim Good

Grilled Halibut with Lemon and Basil

Take a big slab of halibut, grill it to perfection. Melt 1/2 stick of butter together with 1/2 cup of fresh basil and add in fresh lemon juice from 2 lemons. Set aside.

Flash boil or steam fresh green beans (in an active geyser if you can, or just a pot if you aren't in Iceland or Yellowstone). Stack these next to the halibut. Pour the lemon/basil/ butter sauce over the fish and beans, then rush it to the table and eat it.

Icelandic Rye Bread with Butter

Find Icelandic rye bread (Rúgbrauð). The real thing should be cooked in a pot or steamed in a wooden container buried in the ground near a hot spring. If you can't do that, just buy some dense dark rye bread from the store. Serve with butter.

Shots of Brinniven

This should be self-explanatory. Any brand you can find will work. The clear alcohol should cut the overall amount of butter on the table a bit, and will remind you of the frailty of life in a harsh climate. Happily reflect on the fact that fermented shark (another Icelandic specialty) is not being served as you down the fiery shots of Brinniven. You may also need some natural springwater with this, but that is up to you.

No-Bake Skyr Cake

Buy a big tub of vanilla skyr (Icelandic yoghurt). Any brand will work – 16 oz. is enough. Get a box of ginger snaps and a box of vanilla wafers. Get 16 oz of heavy whipping cream. Find some fresh blueberries, raspberries, or if possible, cloudberries.

THE CRUST

Get a spring-form pan like those you use for cheesecake. Put the paper in the bottom to keep it from sticking. Take 1/2 cup of crushed vanilla wafers and mix in 1/2 cup of crushed ginger snaps in a bowl. Add in 1/4 cup of dark brown sugar and mix it all up. Stir in a melted stick of butter.

Pour this mixture into the bottom of the spring-form pan and press it down with your fingers to an even floor over the entire bottom of the pan. Anything from 1/4" to 3/8" thick is fine (but try for the 1/4"- it really is enough). Put the whole pan with the crust in place in the fridge while you whip the cream and mix up the filling.

THE FILLING

Put a heavy bowl, beaters or whisk, and the heavy whipping cream into the freezer for 30 minutes. Having everything really cold will help in whipping the cream.

In the now frosty bowl, pour in the whipping cream. Add in 2 tablespoons of powdered sugar, and 1/2 tsp pure vanilla extract. Whip it up. If a few ice crystals have formed, don't worry, they'll warm back up.

Once stiff peaks are forming in the whipped cream, gently stir in the skyr. Mix it up. Pour this mixture into the spring-form pan and level it up.

Add fresh blueberries (or whatever berries you like – particularly cloudberries if you can find them). Put the whole thing back into the refrigerator and wait a few hours before serving.

RIGHT: ILLUSTRATION BY JIM GOOD

a shot of Brennivin!

Hallgrimskirkja salt

Hekla volcano pepper

Mm hmm... grilled halibut w/lemon & basil, green beans, rye bread & skyr cake.

Jim Good (TUSA 1981)

I started out as a real architect-to-be in New Orleans, Louisiana where I was born. After graduation from the Tulane School of Architecture in 1981 I worked briefly in the office of Barron & Toups as a draftsman and then went to the US Peace Corps and served in the Philippines for 2 years. I came back to the US and ended up working for a short time as a private architect in a small firm in Madison, Wisconsin (Kieth Brink & Associates). After being laid off there, I moved on to a staff architect position with the University of Wisconsin. After a few years there, and the threat of being "groomed for management", I jumped back into private architectural practice in another small office as a Partner with Thompson & Good.

From that perch I became involved with international response to emergencies as an emergency shelter specialist. In time I became involved with refugee emergency response and have worked extensively with the UN High Commission for Refugees (and others) in the wider study of disaster management and coordination of international humanitarian response across the technical sectors.

While I retain my architecture license, I rarely-use it, but do depend on my architectural training almost daily. I now have 32 years of experience in the disaster management field and a long record of designing and delivering training programs in emergency and disaster response for UN agencies, NGO's, and national governments. Throughout it all, I continue to draw and sketch and make little watercolors in my black books.

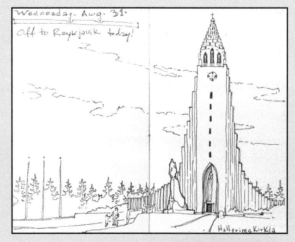

DRAWING BY JIM GOOD

Easy Red Beans and Rice

1 BAG OF DRIED RED BEANS
(CAMELIA BRAND IF YOU CAN GET IT)

1 ENTIRE BUNCH (ALL THE STALKS) OF CELERY

2 BIG SMOKED SAUSAGES

4 BIG BAY LEAVES (OR 7 LITTLE ONES)

SALT & BLACK PEPPER

GUMBO FILET (OPTIONAL)

ORIGINAL TABASCO SAUCE

1 TBSP BROWN SUGAR

LONG GRAINED WHITE RICE

1. Put the dried red beans into a big pot with water, washing them well, and sorting out any weevilly beans, gravel, mud bits, or any other items that aren't good red beans.

2. Set these aside in a covered pot for one day. If you want these for Monday night, start your preps on Saturday night.

3. On Sunday night, drain off the brownish bean water, and flush it with clear water until only clear water runs through. Put these on to cook in a very big pot (you are going to be adding a lot of volume to this).

4. Take out the whole bunch of celery and wash it well, cut off the butt and throw it away. Dice the remaining celery up into very small pieces (about 1/4" slices) and add it into the pot (do include the leaves).

5. On the same cutting board, chop up your smoked sausages. I cut mine on the diagonal at about 1/2" slices, but preferences vary on size and shape of the sausage bits. It is only important that you put 2 whole smoked sausages in there, cut up to your preference.

6. If you have the big bay leaves, put the 4 leaves in at the edge of the pot, one at each cardinal point of the compass (for improved mojo – or as some would have it – good chi). If your bay leaves are small, put in seven (for luck) – spaced equally around the pot.

7. Cook it at a slow boiling heat for several hours. The celery should begin to melt into the sauce, the beans should start collapsing and the skins will curl up when you blow on them.

8. Taste it. At this point, add in the Tabasco to your own taste, add the spoonful of brown sugar, and a heavy dose of salt and black pepper. Stir it and keep tasting and tweaking the salt, pepper, and Tabasco until it tastes right. Once it tastes right, take it off the stove and set it aside until 2 hours before dinner time the next day (once it cools you can put it in the fridge).

9. At 2 hours before dinner time on Monday, heat it up again. Stir it and see how thick it is. If it is too runny after cooking for an additional hour, add a tbsp of Gumbo Filet as a thickener. (It also adds a slightly muddy taste that a lot of people like, so you can add this even if the viscosity is OK).

10. At 1 hour before dinner time on Monday, start the rice.

11. Serve it up. At dinner time, serve out the hot rice in big soup bowls, and ladle in the RB&R.

12. Beer is the right thing to drink with this in all seasons.

Le Corbusier

LA CHAUX-DE-FONDS, SWITZERLAND
1887 - 1965

TULANE CONTRIBUTOR

Nancy Scheinholtz

TUSA 1980

LE CORBUSIER'S VILLA SAVOYE (POISSY, FRANCE) PHOTO BY NANCY SCHEINHOLTZ

LE CORBUSIER was a Swiss-French architect, urban planner, artist, furniture designer, writer, and a true pioneer of modern architecture. His career spanned five decades and his work can be seen all over the world. I have had the pleasure of visiting three Corbu buildings — Villa Roche, Paris, 1923, Villa Savoye in Poissy 1928-1931, and Ronchamp 1950-55. I unearthed travel notes from my trip to Ronchamp:

"This visit is probably the most anticipation I have ever had to see a building. From the winding mountain road, I could catch glimpses of the white towers against the blue sky in the distance. As we neared on foot, classical music could be heard but not a peek of the building. Gregorian chants were playing loud and clear and a very spiritual feeling evolved from the setting and the expectation of the masterpiece beyond. And then, all at once, the entire building appeared commanding total focus. It changed with every step. The plasticity of its form and its sculptural beauty had me gasping. I couldn't speak. I could only move around it, seeing each changing façade. The music continued, then the bells tolled. Inside, the light filtered through the deep fenestration spreading color thru the chapel. The white-washed tower soared. It amazed me that such simple materials—glass and concrete—could be so beautiful."

- Nancy Scheinholtz (TUSA 1980)

LE CORBUSIER'S CHAPELLE NOTRE DAME DU HAUT (RONCHAMP, FRANCE) PHOTO BY NANCY SCHEINHOLTZ

Le Corbusier | Dinner Party

MAIN COURSE
Confit Byaldi (Ratatouille)

DRINK
Corbu Cocktail

"BUSTE DE FEMME," LE CORBUSIER, 1964

CONFIT BIYALDI (RATATOUILLE) WITH PASTRY HAND
PLATING DESIGN BY NANCY SCHEINHOLTZ

Corbu Cocktail

LILLET BLANC

SPLASH OF ELDERFLOWER TONIC

TWIST OF ORANGE

SPRIG OF MINT

Serve very cold and enjoy.

Confit Byaldi (Ratatouille)

6 LARGE ROMA TOMATOES

2 RED BELL PEPPERS

1 CUP VEGETABLE STOCK

2 TBSP FRESH ROSEMARY

1 TSP THYME

1 GARLIC CLOVE

1 SMALL ONION

3 TBSP OLIVE OIL

KOSHER SALT & FRESHLY GROUND PEPPER

2 MEDIUM ZUCCHINI

2 MEDIUM YELLOW SQUASH

2 JAPANESE EGGPLANTS

COARSELY CHOPPED ITALIAN PARSLEY

Blanch and peel the tomatoes. Roast/blacken, peel and seed the red peppers. Slice the zucchini, squash, eggplant, and four of the tomatoes into 1/8" slices, using a mandoline on all but the tomatoes.

Chop and sautee the onion. Chop and add the vegetable scraps along with the stock, two tomatoes, roasted red peppers, garlic, thyme, and 1 TBSP rosemary, 1 TBSP of the olive oil and a pinch of salt. When all are softened, blend in a blender or food processor.

Preheat the oven to 225°. Evenly spread a thin layer of the roasted pepper mixture on the bottom of a shallow casserole. Start with the eggplant, followed with a slice of tomato, slice of yellow squash, and the zucchini, begin layering the sliced vegetables around the outer edge overlapping 1/4" between slices. Layer until you reach the center of the casserole.

Chop the remaining rosemary and sprinkle on top. Drizzle 1 TBSP of olive oil and sprinkle with salt and pepper.

Cut a piece of parchment with a hole to fit on top of the vegetables. Roast for about 1 hour and 30 minutes; remove the parchment after 1 hour and 10 minutes. The vegetables should be completely softened but still hold their shape.

Place a ring mold in the center of a large plate and fill it with vegetables stacked vertically. Place a layer of vegetables staggered horizontally over the top. Combine the red pepper sauce from the bottom of the casserole with the remaining TBSP of olive oil, then drizzle it in a circle around the outside of the vegetable stack. Garnish with the parsley and serve. Voila!

TULANE CONTRIBUTOR

Nancy Scheinholtz (TUSA 1980)

Scheinholtz Associates is a design-oriented architectural firm established in 1985. Handling primarily residential construction, the firm has a unique ability to work within the Bay Area's intricate building process to create projects that are compatible with the client and community. Personal involvement guides each project, from neighborhood meetings to public hearings to building codes. We work on both traditional and contemporary homes. The clients tell us their image of the home and we enhance their vision. The unifying element in our work is clean, well-designed spaces.

The photos shown here are of a recently-completed project. It was a marriage of a trusting client, skilled contractor, and a lot of hard work. www.scheinholtzassociates.com

ABOVE: BACKYARD VIEW OF A NEW MODERN HOME IN HILLSBOROUGH, CALIFORNIA
RIGHT: CORNER FIREPLACE WITH CANTILEVERED CONCRETE HEARTH WHICH TURNS INTO STAIR
TREAD, MILLWORK FOLLOWS THE CONCRETE MANTLE AS DOES THE STONE WALL.
DESIGNED BY NANCY SCHEINHOLTZ.

Gertrude Sawyer

TUSCOLA, ILLINOIS
1895 - 1996

Michael Bolster

TUSA 1980

TUDOR HALL RESTORATION (LEONARDTOWN, MD) DESIGNED BY GERTRUDE SAWYER

Born in Tuscola, Illinois, GERTRUDE SAWYER turned back all efforts to thwart her from realizing a dream to become an architect. She began with a Bachelor's degree in Landscape Architecture from the University of Illinois in 1918, then pushed on to earn a Master's degree in architecture through the Cambridge School of Architecture at Smith College in 1922. Wasting no time, she designed her first house in 1922 and had it built and sold it within a year. In 1923, Gertrude moved to Washington, D.C. to work in the office of well-known architect Horace Peaslee, eventually striking out on her own shortly thereafter. In 1934 she was hired by US Tax Court Judge J. E. Murdock to design a new house for his family in a spa-cious lot north of Georgetown. An interesting choice of architect by conservative Judge Murdock, but, by all accounts, complete satisfaction reigned. Known for her mastery of the Colonial Revival style, she bestowed the Judge's Foxhall Road residence with her considerable detailing skills and was responsible for the landscape design as well. She was an excellent draftsperson, producing pencil-on-vellum renderings worthy of framing. Judge Murdock was my grandfather and I spent several formative summers in his house. I give complete credit to Gertrude's exceptional creation as inspiration for my professional life.

- *Michael Bolster (TUSA 1980)*

COUNTRY CLUB (KANSAS CITY, MO) DESIGNED BY GERTRUDE SAWYER

| Gertrude Sawyer | Luncheon |

MAIN COURSE
Cucumber Sandwiches

DRINK
Sun Tea with Lemon

Gertrude maintained a practice until 1969. She retired and moved to Pasadena, California. My older sister schooled at nearby Scripps College and was a frequent guest of Gertrude's in the mid '70's. With Victorian flair, Gertrude often presented this simple luncheon fare with iced glasses of sun-made tea with lemon. The greens and lemons were fresh from her garden.

- Michael Bolster (TUSA 1980)

MICHAEL BOLSTER'S GRANDFATHER'S HOUSE, WASHINGTON, D.C. (DESIGNED BY GETRUDE SAWYER)

Cucumber Sandwiches

Deftly remove the crust from thin slices of white bread. Ease a slim layer of mayonnaise onto the crustless bread. Gently lay fresh sprigs of watercress across the bread face. Top with fresh slices of cucumber, taking care to place one in each quadrant. Top with another bread slice, also graced with mayonnaise. Cut into equal squares. Serve on appropriately sized china.

Sun Tea with Lemon

In a one gallon water dispenser, place 8 bags of tea in cool water. A nice blend of green tea, hibiscus and peach makes for a satisfyingly rich color and fruity taste. Cover and set container in the sun for 2-3 hours, depending on preferred strength. Add honey to taste, stirring in ¼ cup at a time to desired sweetness. Finally add sliced lemon for a light citrus addition. Refrigeration lends a refreshing briskness to the beverage.

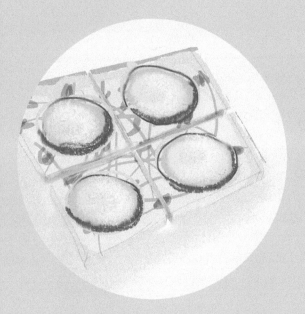

ILLUSTRATIONS BY MICHAEL BOLSTER

TULANE CONTRIBUTOR

Michael Bolster (TUSA 1980)

Following our graduation, I moved to England for a spell before heading to the Yemen Arab Republic for four years. In Yemen, I worked as a Peace Corps volunteer and for an NGO installing rural water systems. Returning to the US, I eventually ended up in the office of Robert AM Stern. I hung my own shingle in 1987 with a practice focused on private residences.

Projects in France, Florida, New York, New Jersey, Chicago, Michigan, California, Massachusetts, Connecticut & Wisconsin have kept me busy. At some point, a Master's degree materialized out of thin air. I currently live in Janesville, Wisconsin, with my wife Sukey Ryan. Our only child, Henry, lives in Washington, DC

DIGITAL RENDERING ABOVE AND PHOTOS ON RIGHT BY MICHAEL BOLSTER

Blue Pecan Swirl

Fill the basin of a handmade, hand-turned, kaolin-clay-based porcelain bowl with three generous scoops of organic, Northern Caucus, whole milk kefir.

To that add a large handful of frozen, western-slope, hand-picked Michigan blueberries, randomly sprinkled atop the kefir. Best to know actual picker.

Next, carefully sprinkle amongst the blueberries a bunch of wild-harvested, unsalted, sprouted, raw, unsprayed, unpasteurized, organic pecans.

Now place the filled bowl on a suitably-sized saucer of equal provenance. Onto the rim of the saucer, artfully arrange a series of quartered, peel-on, unbruised miniature Rockit ™ apples from Chelan Valley, Washington.

Bean Whirlwind

Steam French beans (Haricots Verts) and sliced Moldovan zucchini. Set aside.

Make a salad of snipped Asian pea shoot microgreens, diced Argentinian apples, chopped English red cabbage and cut Chilean pears.

Make a salad dressing of Spanish olive oil, toasted Egyptian sesame oil, Modena balsamic vinegar, Chungcheong rice vinegar, Dijon mustard, vegan Worcestershire sauce, Thai sriracha sauce and Greek-style yoghurt. Mix thoroughly and pour over salad.

"Swirl" the string beans around the salad and place the zucchini around the edge.

Place two slices of roasted Hengstenberg beets on top of the salad.

Lay two strips of preserved Slovakian mackerel over the beets.

Head to McDonald's.

NOTABLE ARCHITECT

Luis Barragán

GUADALAJARA, MEXICO
1902 - 1988

CONTRIBUTOR

Virginia Walcott

COOKBOOK DESIGNER (1994 -)

CUADRA SAN CRISTÓBAL (MEXICO CITY, MEXICO) DESIGNED BY LUIS BARRAGÁN

The works of LUIS BARRAGÁN seem to slow down time. An expert in space, form, and the way they interact to affect our emotions, the architect and civil engineer used tools like landscape design, bold blocks of color, and natural elements to create structures that played with the reality of their surrounding environment. Much of his work asks us to consider the sentimental versus functional purpose of the home; according to Barragán, "Any work of architecture which does not express serenity is a mistake."

The works of Le Corbusier and European modernists greatly influenced his practice, but the way he adapted these trends is especially unique. Barragán worked without great fame for much of his career until the Museum of Modern Art presented a retrospective of his work in 1975. In 1980, he was awarded the Pritzker Prize, only the second in the award's history. He died in Mexico City at eighty-three years old.

- *Virginia Walcott*

CASA LUIS BARRAGÁN (MEXICO CITY, MEXICO) DESIGNED BY LUIS BARRAGÁN

| Luis Barragán | Dinner Party |

SOUP
Pozole Verde

DRINK
Cazuela

DESSERT
Jericalla

Pozole Verde

7 CUPS CHICKEN STOCK OR
LOW-SODIUM BROTH

2 CUPS WATER

4 CHICKEN BREAST HALVES ON
THE BONE, WITH SKIN

1 LB TOMATILLOS, HUSKED AND HALVED

1 SMALL ONION, QUARTERED

2 POBLANO CHILES, CORED, SEEDED
AND QUARTERED

2 JALAPEÑOS, SEEDED AND QUARTERED

4 LARGE GARLIC CLOVES, SMASHED

1/2 CUP CHOPPED CILANTRO

1 TBSP OREGANO LEAVES

SALT AND PEPPER

1 TBSP VEGETABLE OIL

3 15-OZ. CANS OF HOMINY, DRAINED

FOR SERVING: SLICED RADISHES, CHOPPED ONION, DICED
AVOCADO, SOUR CREAM, TORTILLA CHIPS, LIME WEDGES

In a large, enameled cast-iron pot, bring the chicken stock and water to a boil. Add the chicken breasts, skin side down. Cover and simmer over very low heat until they're tender and cooked through (about 25 minutes). Transfer the chicken breasts to a plate and shred the meat. Discard the bones and skin. Skim any fat from the cooking liquid and save.

In a blender, combine the halved tomatillos with the quartered onion, poblanos and jalapeños, smashed garlic, chopped cilantro, and oregano. Pulse until coarsely chopped, scraping down the sides. With the machine on, add 1 cup of the cooking liquid and puree until smooth. Season the tomatillo puree with salt and pepper.

In a large, deep skillet, heat the vegetable oil until it shimmers. Add the tomatillo puree and cook over medium heat. Stir occasionally until the sauce turns a deep green, about 12 minutes.

Pour the green sauce into the cooking liquid in the cast-iron pot. Add the hominy and bring to a simmer over medium heat. Add the shredded chicken to the stew, season with salt and pepper, and cook just until heated through. Serve the pozole in deep bowls and garnish as directed.

Adapted from Food & Wine

BARRAGÁN OUTDOOR DINING DESIGN (ILLUSTRATED BY VIRGINIA WALCOTT)

Jericalla

1 1/2 QUARTS MILK

2 CINNAMON STICKS

1 TSP VANILLA EXTRACT
(MEXICAN VANILLA PREFERRED)

1 1/2 CUPS SUGAR

8 EGG YOLKS

Boil milk and cinnamon sticks together in a saucepan. Stir constantly to avoid scorching. Reduce heat, simmer for 10 minutes, then add vanilla. Remove from heat and cool. Stir in sugar and cook over low heat, stirring occasionally, for 30 minutes. Remove from heat and cool. Meanwhile, beat egg yolks and add to cooled milk mixture. Preheat oven to 350°F.

Divide mixture among 8 heat-resistant dessert dishes or ramekins. Bake in a water bath for 30 to 35 minutes or until a toothpick inserted into the center of the custard comes out clean. Brown under broiler for 3 to 5 minutes or until tops are golden (or use a Crème Brûlée torch). Refrigerate for 2 hours and un-mold onto dessert plates.

Adapted from Food.com

Cazuela

JUICE FROM 1 GRAPEFRUIT

JUICE FROM 2 ORANGES

JUICE FROM 2-3 LIMES

3-4 CUPS OF TEQUILA BLANCO

FRESH CUT SLICES OF ORANGES, GRAPEFRUIT, LIME (ONE OF EACH)

JARRITOS OR OTHER GRAPEFRUIT SODA (ABOUT 5-6 CUPS)

ICE

SALT, CHILE SPICE (OPTIONAL)

Combine all the ingredients in a large bowl. Serve the drink in a cazuela or other shallow dish with a straw. Dust the rim of each dish with salt and chile.

Adapted from The Tipsy Gypsies

CONTRIBUTOR

Virginia Walcott

Virginia Walcott is an artist, designer, and filmmaker from the Gulf Coast of Alabama. She is the designer of this book, an idea her dad (Mac Walcott, pages 58, 94) pitched to her at the beginning of the pandemic. Virginia graduated from the University of Pennsylvania in 2016 and has spent the last five years working for publications like *The Atlantic* and *Scalawag Magazine*. Her art practice focuses on 2D/3D mixed media and video, looking at topics such as our natural, built, and digital environments, ideas of home, and the U.S. South. She lives in New Orleans where she teaches at various art centers and runs a commercial studio called Superhumid, working with clients primarily in journalism and music. She and her dad share a love of starting too many creative projects for their own good.

FAVORITE RECIPE

Oatmeal Chocolate Chip Butterscotch Cookies

2 STICKS OF BUTTER, MELTED	1 TSP BAKING SODA
1 CUP FIRMLY PACKED BROWN SUGAR	1 TSP GROUND CINNAMON
1/2 CUP GRANULATED SUGAR	1/2 TSP SALT
2 EGGS	3 CUPS QUICK OR OLD FASHIONED OATS
1 TSP VANILLA	1 CUP SEMI-SWEET CHOCOLATE CHIPS
1 1/2 CUPS ALL-PURPOSE FLOUR	1 CUP BUTTERSCOTCH CHIPS

Heat oven to 350°F. In large bowl, beat butter and sugars until creamy. Add eggs and vanilla; beat well. Add flour, baking soda, cinnamon and salt; mix well. Add oats, chocolate chips, and butterstock chips. Mix well. Drop dough by rounded table-spoonfuls onto ungreased cookie sheets. Bake 8 to 10 minutes or until light golden brown. Cool 1 minute on cookie sheets; remove to wire rack. Store tightly covered.

Adapted from Quaker Oats

STILLS FROM "QUIET AS A MOUSE" (2020)
WRITTEN AND PERFORMED BY KATE KELLY
DIRECTED, FILMED, AND EDITED BY VIRGINIA WALCOTT
NEW ORLEANS FILM FESTIVAL OFFICIAL SELECTION 2020

NOTABLE ARCHITECT

A. Hays Town

CROWLEY, LOUISIANA
1903 - 2005

TULANE CONTRIBUTOR

Mac Walcott

TUSA 1980

In the summer of 1972, my best friend's family began "fixing up" an old house down the street from us. We lived in an older part of Greenville, Mississippi on a main street populated by grand old homes of all styles, mostly built in the early 1900's. I remember coming home and telling my parents about the cool leaded glass windows, pecky cypress paneling, old beams, dipped doors, and restored hardware they were using in their "renovation," (the newer, upscale word for "fixing up"). My parents, who were as frugal as any depression-era couple, easily appreciated the economics of re-using old materials, but weren't at all keen yet on the aesthetic value of these old artifacts.

Only now do I see the connection between the curious renovation of my friend's tired home and the movement started by Hays Town in the 1960's. While modernism has given us the technology and mindsets to easily and willfully destroy our architectural heritages, Hays Town began a narrative that perfected the concept of rescuing these old artifacts and celebrating them in an appropriate vernacular context.

ALBERT HAYS TOWN was born in Crowley, Louisiana, in 1903. He received his B.S. in Architecture from Tulane in 1924. He went to work for N. W. Overstreet Architect in Jackson, Mississippi in 1926, becoming a partner in 1932. During the heyday of the firm, they designed many of the modernist courthouse, schools, and other civic buildings throughout the state of Mississippi. Their Bailey High School was featured on the cover of Time Magazine. In 1939, Hays moved to Baton Rouge and started his own firm. While in his mid-sixties, his empathy for traditional Louisiana architecture led him to convert his practice to residential-only projects. He cultivated in-depth relationships with his clients and their detailed choices within their homes. He is believed to have completed over 1,000 projects. He practiced until he was 95 and died in 2005, aged 101.

- *Mac Walcott (TUSA 1980)*

LEFT AND ABOVE: RESIDENCE (BATON ROUGE, LA) DESIGNED BY A. HAYS TOWN

A. Hays Town	Dinner Party

SOUP
Potage Pintar

APPETIZER
Fried Asparagus

MAIN COURSE
Sauteed Shrimp and Okra

DRINK
Syllabub

In imagining what Mr. Town might enjoy, I took a look at some of the old recipe books on our shelves from the 1930's and 40's. The canned ingredients found there were a surprise, but I suspect these items were then considered modern and smart.

- Mac Walcott

Potage Pintar

1 TBSP FLOUR

2 TSP BUTTER

1 PINT CONDENSED MILK, HEATED (CAN SUBSTITUTE REAL MILK)

1/2 CUP PEANUT BUTTER (CRUNCHY IF YOU WANT SOME TEXTURE)

SALT TO TASTE

1/2 SHOT DRY SHERRY

Melt the butter in a small skillet and make a quick roux with the flour. Add the hot milk slowly, and whisk till smooth. Add the peanut butter a small dollop at a time, blend as you go. To serve, add the sherry and a heaping teaspoon of whipped cream per serving. Serves four. It has a very delicate touch.

"He carries the same weight as Frank Loyd Wright around here... He contributed to our culture for a very long time. It's why he's so relevant. His houses persist."

Ursula Emery, A. Hays Town Professor, LSU School of Architecture

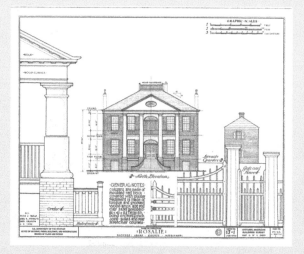

Fried Asparagus

1 CAN OF ASPARAGUS

FLOUR

BREAD CRUMBS

BEATEN EGG

SALT AND BLACK PEPPER

Drain and dry the asparagus stalks. Lightly sprinkle with salt and pepper to taste, then dip in flour, dip in beaten egg, and finally, dip in bread crumbs. Fry in hot peanut oil. Drain and eserve with dollop (to side) of Hellman's real mayonnaise for dipping

Sauteed Shrimp and Okra

This is a very simple, flexible dish. Combine equal parts of raw, peeled shrimp with raw, cut okra. Shrimp can be cut in half to help with texture. Brown shrimp and okra together in butter, using two tablespoons of butter for every cup of shrimp/okra mix. Add salt and pinches of black, white, and red pepper to taste while the mixture browns. Should take about 10 minutes. Turn several times while browning. Cook until okra is tender and brown, and shrimps are just done. If mixture is too dry when cooking, add 1/4 cup splashes of water, broth, or red wine as needed and cook until reduced. Serve over buttered grits cooked in chicken broth.

Syllabub

2 CUPS HEAVY CREAM

2 EGG WHITES

1 CUP POWDERED SUGAR

5 TBSP SHERRY, BRANDY, OR MADEIRA WINE

2 TBSP LEMON JUICE

1 TBSP POWDERED SUGAR TO TOP

VARIOUS FRUIT COMBINATIONS, 1/2 CUP: SLICED BANANAS, PEACHES CUT INTO PIECES, DICED PINEAPPLE, OR SATSUMAS CUT INTO SMALL PIECES

This classic southern dessert was sometimes thought to begin a young southerner's journey into alcoholism. It is so mild that is was often served to children, which was thought to initiate their taste (and desire) for liquor. Hmm.

Take 1/2 cup of the powdered sugar and whip with the cream until stiff. Take the other 1/2 cup of powdered sugar and beat with the egg white stiffly in another bowl. Combine the two mixtures well while stirring lightly. Add the wine or other liquor and then pour over the fruit mixtures placed in the bottom of a bowl, or in individual servings. Let it stand for a few minutes while you sip leftover liquor or wine. Top with lemon juice and powdered sugar dust to taste.

TULANE CONTRIBUTOR

Mac Walcott (TUSA 1980)

Carswell M. (Mac) Walcott is a 1980 graduate of the Tulane University School of Architecture. In 2004, he miraculously received his Masters degree from Tulane. He and his wife, Gina, are founding principals of Walcott Adams Verneuille Architects in Fairhope, Alabama. They live on Fish River at Little House Farms where he longs to be a literate farmer like Wendell Berry or Noel Perrin. The "literate" and "farmer" continue to elude him.

FAVORITE RECIPE

Sally's Shrimp Kumquat

2 TBSP BUTTER

1 CUP HALF AND HALF

2 CUPS FRESH SHRIMP STOCK

1 LB SHRIMP, HEADS ON

4 LARGE LEMONS, JUICED

6 KUMQUATS, QUARTERED, REMOVE SEEDS

1 TSP KOSHER SALT

1/2 TSP BLACK PEPPER

1/2 TSP WHITE PEPPER

1/2 TSP RED PEPPER

CHOPPED GREEN ONIONS FOR GARNISH

1 CUP BROWN RICE, COOKED IN SHRIMP STOCK

For some odd reason, Hurricane Sally spared our citrus trees, and they came through the storm with hardly a limb broken and with a nice surprise bounty of intact fruit amongst the ruins. This recipe was made up just last weekend, when Gina brought in a basket full of lemons, limes, and kumquats from our trees.

Peel and head the shrimp, rinse shrimp and set aside. Place shells and heads in pot in 2 1/2 cups of water, add salt. Cover pot and bring to a soft boil for 30 minutes. Strain to make 2+ cups of fresh shrimp stock. Use 1 cup for the recipe, 1 cup for brown rice.

Melt the butter, add the half and half, mix together. Slowly stir in lemon juice, mix until simmering, blended well, and reduce until it starts to thicken. Add spices, shrimp, and kumquats, simmer until shrimps are just done. Serve over mound of brown rice. Add whole kumquat to top.

RIGHT: BYRNE CHAPEL (FAIRHOPE, AL)
OPPOSITE PAGE | TOP: FAIRHOPE PUBLIC LIBRARY (FAIRHOPE, AL) BOTTOM: CHRIST EPISCOPAL CHURCH (BAY ST. LOUIS, MS)
ALL DESIGNED BY MAC WALCOTT

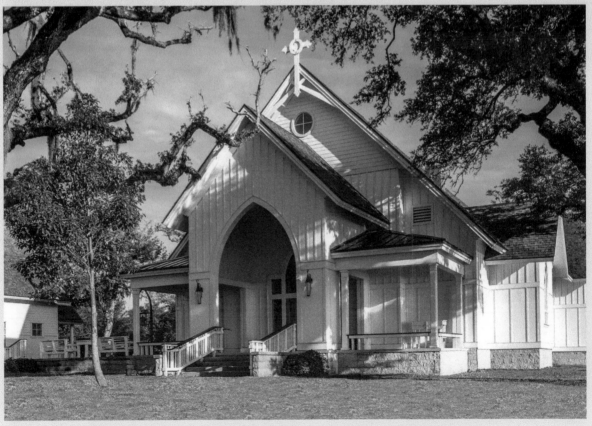

NOTABLE ARCHITECT

Carlo Scarpa

VENICE, ITALY
1906 - 1978

TULANE CONTRIBUTOR

Susan Regan

TUSA 1980

"An artist must create an optic, a way of seeing nature like it's never been seen before."

"If the architecture is any good, a person who looks and listens will feel its good effects without noticing."

- CARLO SCARPA

• Born and spent his life in the Veneto region of Italy with a love for Japan and friends around the globe.

• Apprenticed with architect Francesco Rinaldo and studied architectural drawing at the Royal Academy of Fine Arts in Venice.

• Director of the Venini Glassworks from 1932 - 1947. Dozens of commissions in and around Venice: private homes and public buildings... many renovations of ancient sites and structures.

• Creator with a 4,000 book library. Maker of beautiful drawings to seed collaborative craft: glass, furniture, and harmonious places layered with elegant texture and detail... serenissima & shibui

- *Susan Regan (TUSA 1980)*

LEFT AND ABOVE: BRION TOMB (TREVISO, ITALY) DESIGNED BY CARLO SCARPA

Carlo Scarpa	Desserts

Scarpagrappa Truffles

6 OUNCES DARK CHOCOLATE

1/2 CUP HEAVY CREAM

1 TBSP SUPERFINE SUGAR

1/2 CUP GRAPPA

COCOA DUST

Chop chocolate into small bits and set aside in a bowl. Mix cream and sugar, bring to a boil, pour over chocolate... adding grappa. Let stand 6 minutes until melted and mix until smooth; cool to room temperature before refrigerating for 2 hours or so. Scoop balls, finger smooth, and place on a wax paper-lined tray. Refrigerate. Roll the balls in dust and serve one or two with an espresso for an enhanced pick me up.

Six Layer Tiramicarlo

3 FRESH SOURCE-SCREENED EGGS, SEPARATED

1/2 CUP SUPERFINE SUGAR

8 OUNCES MASCARPONE

1 1/2 CUPS STRONG BLACK COFFEE, COOLED

2 TBSP+ NOCELLO LIQUOR FROM BOLOGNA

24 SAVOIARDI BISCUITS

COCOA DUST

You'll need 2 bowls, a coffee vessel, a hand mixer, a loaf pan, and a refrigerator.

Beat (speed 6) egg yolks with sugar for 10 minutes. Add 1 TBSP coffee and mascarpone; beat just enough to combine. Set aside.

Beat (speed 6) egg whites for 3 minutes. Very gently fold in half the mascarpone mixture; fold in the balance. Mix the liquor into the coffee. Quickly dip each of the 8 biscuits, one side at a time, to make the first layer in the pan. Add 1/3 of mascarpone mixture. Repeat and repeat.

Cover to refrigerate for at least 6 hours - time enough to get waivers from all who'll partake that they know and agree it has raw egg.

Dust with cocoa; serve on a chilled glass plate with an elegant implement. Recommended accompaniment: Amarone della Valpolicella (red wine).

RECIPES HENKŌ AND ILLUSTRATIONS BY SUSAN REGAN

TULANE CONTRIBUTOR

Susan Regan (TUSA 1980)

Registered Architect since 1989 | Chicago's North Shore
www.runnercollective.com | Spaces | Susan Regan

Canapé creative collaborator: Jonathon McKnight
McKnight + Partners, Inc. | General Contractors | Evanston, IL

FAVORITE RECIPE

McSue's Avocado + Gorgonzola Deconstructed Canapés

BREMNER WAFERS

FRESH RIPE AVOCADOS

GORGONZOLA CHEESE

MCILHENNY TABASCO GREEN PEPPER SAUCE

Prepare site. Slice, crumble, souse with sauce, and fork load onto wafers. Demolish with tumblers of Elijah Craig Kentucky Bourbon on the rocks with Luxardo maraschino cherries.

ABOVE: PHOTO BY SUSAN REGAN
RIGHT: GARDEN AT THE QUERINI STAMPALIA, DESIGNED BY CARLO SCARPA

Shreve, Lamb & Harmon

NEW YORK, NEW YORK
1929 - 1971

Carson Kapp

TUSA 1980

The Empire State Building coined its name from "Empire State," the nickname for the state of New York, and was designed in an Art Deco style by SHREVE, LAMB & HARMON. In a New York competition to make it the "world's tallest building," the design changed 15 times, including structural setbacks of the upper floors, adding 5 floors and a spire. The building became a symbol of prosperity and promise. With its roof height of 1,250 feet and total building height (including its antenna) of 1,454 feet, it remained the tallest until 1970 when the World Trade Center was completed. After the World Trade Center collapse on September 11, 2001, the Empire State building again became New York's tallest skyscraper until 2012.

Originally, the site was an 18th-century farm. In 1893, the site housed the Waldorf Astoria Hotel. This icon was not only named as one of the "Seven Wonders of the Modern World" by the American Society of Civil Engineers, but ranked first as "America's Favorite Architecture" by the American Institute of Architects in 2007. Named as a city landmark in 1980 by the New York City Landmarks Preservation Commission, it was added as well to the National Register of Historic Places as a National Historic Landmark in 1986.

Many movies including "King Kong" and "An Affair to Remember" (also the name of my painting inspired by Cary Grant and Deborah Kerr) along with 250 TV shows included this American Icon and symbol of New York City as a backdrop. Even though there was favorable publicity, the owners did not make a profit until the early 1950's due to the Great Depression and World War II.

- *Carson Kapp (TUSA 1980)*

LEFT AND ABOVE: EMPIRE STATE BUILDING (NEW YORK, NY)
DESIGNED BY SHREVE, LAMB & HARMON

Shreve, Lamb & Harmon | Dinner Party

APPETIZER
Oysters Rockefeller

SALAD
Waldorf Salad

MAIN COURSE
Manhattan Clam Chowder

ILLUSTRATIONS BY CARSON KAPP

Oysters Rockefeller

1 MEDIUM ONION, FINELY CHOPPED

1/2 CUP BUTTER, CUBED

1 PACKAGE (9 OUNCES) FRESH
SPINACH, TORN

1 CUP GRATED ROMANO CHEESE

1 TBSP LEMON JUICE

1/8 TSP PEPPER

2 POUNDS KOSHER SALT

3 DOZEN FRESH OYSTERS IN THE SHELL, WASHED

GARNISH WITH 3 STRIPS CUT CRISPY BACON

In a large skillet, saute onion in butter until tender. Add spinach, cooking and stirring until wilted. Remove from heat and stir in cheese, lemon juice, and pepper. Spread kosher salt into two ungreased 15x10x1 baking pans. Shuck oysters, reserving oyster and its liquid in the bottom shell. Lightly press oyster shells down into the salt, using salt to keep oysters level. Top each with 2-1/2 tsp. spinach mixture. Bake, uncovered, at 450° until oysters are plump, 6-8 minutes. Top with crispy bacon. Serve immediately.

Adapted from Taste of Home

Waldorf Salad

2 LARGE GALA OR HONEYCRISP APPLES,
UNPEELED AND CHOPPED (ABOUT 3 CUPS)

2 CUPS CHOPPED CELERY

1/4 CUP RAISINS

1/4 CUP CHOPPED WALNUTS, TOASTED

1/3 CUP REDUCED-FAT MAYONNAISE

1/3 CUP PLAIN YOGURT

1/2 CUP RED SEEDLESS GRAPES CUT IN HALF

Combine apples, celery, grapes, raisins and walnuts. Add mayonnaise and yogurt; toss to coat. Refrigerate, covered, until serving. Toast nuts in a shallow pan at 350° oven for 5-10 minutes

Manhattan Clam Chowder

1-1/2 POUNDS POTATOES (ABOUT 3
MEDIUM), PEELED AND CUT INTO
3/4-INCH CUBES

1 LARGE ONION, CHOPPED

2 MEDIUM CARROTS, SHREDDED
(ABOUT 3/4 CUP)

3 CELERY RIBS, SLICED

4 CANS (6-1/2 OUNCES EACH) CHOPPED
CLAMS, UNDRAINED

5 BACON STRIPS, COOKED AND CRUMBLED

1 TBSP DRIED PARSLEY FLAKES

1 BAY LEAF

1-1/2 TSP DRIED THYME

1/4 TSP COARSELY GROUND PEPPER

1 CAN (20 OUNCES) DICED TOMATOES, UNDRAINED

1 CAN (6 OUNCES) TOMATO PASTE

Place all of the ingredients in a four or five quart slow cooker. Cook, covered, on low until vegetables are tender, approximately 7-9 hours. Remove bay leaf before serving.

Adapted from Taste of Home

TULANE CONTRIBUTOR

Carson Kapp (TUSA 1980)

The Orange County Convention Center in Orlando, Florida, is the second largest convention facility in the United States. Carson Kapp was back of house project manager (exhibition space from lobby wall to loading docks, below ground tunnels and catwalks) at Hunton Brady Pryor Maso Architects for the Phase III addition and assisted with Phase IV addition at Helman, Hurley, Charvot and Peacock Architects. Phase III & IV gross square footage of 2,860,400 was the largest project in Carson's career. The height of the Empire State Building fits within the footprint of Phases III & IV.

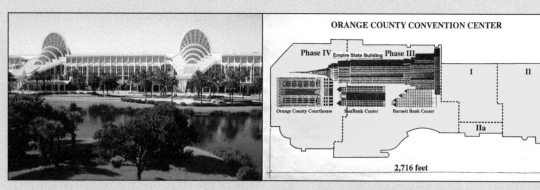

RECIPES, ILLUSTRATIONS, AND PAINTING BY CARSON KAPP

FAVORITE RECIPE

Chicken Marsala

1/4 CUP ALL-PURPOSE FLOUR

1/4 TSP GROUND BLACK PEPPER

1/2 TSP DRIED OREGANO

4 BREAST HALF, SKINLESS, BONELESS CHICKEN BREAST HALVES, POUNDED TO 1/4 INCH THICK

4 TBSP BUTTER

4 TBSP OLIVE OIL

1 CUP SLICED MUSHROOMS

1/2 CUP MARSALA WINE

1/2 CUP COOKING SHERRY

In a shallow bowl, combine the flour, salt, pepper and oregano. Coat the chicken pieces in the flour mixture. In a large skillet, melt butter in the oil over medium heat. Place chicken in the pan and lightly brown. Turn over chicken pieces, and add mushrooms. Pour in wine and sherry. Cover skillet and simmer chicken for 10 minutes, turning once, until no longer pink and juices run clear.

Adapted from Maria Kang

John W. Lawrence

NEW ORLEANS, LOUISIANA
1923 - 1971

Errol Barron

TUSA 1964

MOSSY HOUSE, TERN STREET, LAKE VISTA NEIGHBORHOOD (NEW ORLEANS, LA) DESIGNED BY JOHN LAWRENCE

Though in fact he was young (in his late 30's!), he seemed to me to be a senior player in the word of architecture when I was introduced to him as a high school student by my father, a member of the Dean's Advisory Council in the 1950's. In high school, my interests were clearly focused on architecture and drawing and not much else (as my grades probably showed) so when my Father showed JOHN LAWRENCE some of my drawings and I got an encouraging response, I applied to Tulane hoping to study there as my Father had. (Class of 1918! The year of the great influenza epidemic).

I loathed high school, with its cliquish bands of back biting teens and athletes, and struggled to see the point of some, if not all, of the classes. When Tulane accepted me and I began classes the following fall at TUSA, I was astounded that the work was not only fun but that I seemed to have some aptitude for it. "This is school?" I asked.

Lawrence was a visible presence in the school which was quite small (about 150 students) and though he projected a friendly, if reserved, sense of authority and prestige, he was accessible and encouraging. I took his Professional Concerns class and still remember one of his lines; "The professional is someone with an almost inexhaustible capacity for taking pains."

In the era of high-minded modernism, Lawrence presented a tempered view that modernism, with all its messianic underpinnings, should leave room for an equally important calling to recognize the work of the past and celebrate a more emcompassing, humanistic view of the world than was part of the modernist position generally. No doubt this was in large part because we were in a city with so much good building from the past. New Orleans had a rich cultural heritage that now seems so obvious, but at the time seemed buried under a quest for the future.

In only perhaps 10 years from the date of my graduation in 1964, Lawrence would have appreciated that the whole architectural world, and even the world in general, broadened and deepened to include preservation, cultural inclusivity, social revolution, and societal upheaval, aspects of change ongoing today.

But throughout this period, John W. Lawrence led with a quiet confidence, with a faint smile on his lips and a steely-eyed focus on the importance of design, intelligent planning, and open-minded responses to architectural and social issues. It was a pleasure being a student under such leadership.

- *Errol Barron (TUSA 1964)*

A CONVERSATION WITH JOHN LAWRENCE

11·24·70

John W. Lawrence | RBC Reunion Gumbo

*In the hope that this project will generate future gathering, there will
be a need for sustenance. And this recipe may be just the thing.*

Gumbo Recipe (Chicken and Andouille)
For a party of 12 - 18

12 CHICKEN BREASTS, BONELESS AND SKINLESS

3 1/2 POUNDS OF ANDOUILLE SAUSAGE

2 PACKETS OF SAVOIR DRY ROUX

3 CONTAINERS OF GUIDRIE'S CAJUN TRINITY
(SAVES CUTTING ONIONS, CELERY, AND BELL PEPPERS)

3 CONTAINERS OF ORGANIC CHICKEN STOCK, LOW SODIUM

SALT, PEPPER, AND TABASCO

1 1/2 CUPS OF BURGUNDY RED WINE

1. Cut chicken into 3/4" cubes

2. Put 1/4 cup of olive oil put into a big pot

3. Brown chicken in this pot - do in batches

4. In a second pot filled with water, boil sausages cut into 4-6" long bits for 20 – 25
minutes. When done, jab holes in sausage skin with a sharp knife, then throw the water away.

5. Cut sausages into discs

6. Add olive oil and the containers of stock and roux to second pot. Stir till dissolved.

7. Add everything else including the Guidry Cajun Trinity and the 1 ½ cup of wine

8. Bring all to a boil for 3- 4 minutes then turn down to a simmer - let simmer for 1.5 hours

Serve over rice and with French bread and EAT

Put leftovers into containers and freeze!

INTERIOR, HOUSE DESIGNED BY JOHN W. LAWRENCE IN LAKE TERRACE NEIGHBORHOOD (NEW ORLEANS, LA)

TULANE CONTRIBUTOR

Errol Barron (TUSA 1964)

Errol Barron, FAIA, was the founding partner of Errol Barron / Michael Toups Architects in New Orleans. He has taught design and drawing at Tulane University in New Orleans for 44 years. He is a Fellow in the American Institute of Architecture and was the recipient in 1994 of the Gabriel Prize. In 2012 he was awarded the Gold Medal of the Louisiana Architects Association of the A.I.A. of Louisiana. In 2015, he closed his architecture practice to allow more time for painting and drawing but continues to teach drawing and design. He plays flute in amateur ensembles and released a CD with the pianist Sakiko Ohashi entitled *The Amateur*.

He is the author of 5 books: *Observation – the Architecture, Drawings and Paintings of Errol Barron* (1995); *New Orleans Observed – Drawings and Observations of America's Most Foreign City* (2005); *Roma Osservata / Rome Observed* (2014); *A Tradition of Serenity - The Architecture of Ongard Satrabhandhu* (2015); and *Tulane Observed* (2019). His most recent exhibition, "Reluctant Monuments," was at the Octavia Gallery in New Orleans.

"INDIANOLA" (MIXED MEDIA ON PAPER, 16" X 20") BY ERROL BARRON
FROM THE COLLECTION OF MR. AND MRS. SCOTT HOWARD

MARIANA BAY HOUSE (PELEPONNESOS, GREECE) DESIGNED BY ERROL BARRON

Roasted Chicken

This dish satisfies my innate love of delicious food that requires no expertise or special talent and is a quick solution to the need for a tasty meal when one is hampered by a profound dislike of domestic chores (including preparing elaborate meals). The recipe comes to me from my good friend, the talented history painter George Schmidt. George is a fomer student of John Lawrence (class of '72) but he only completed 3 of the 5 years before transferring to the Art School and getting, instead, a degree in painting. He has subsequently had an outstanding career doing evocative paintings of important historical events from classical Rome to New Orleans Mardi Gras balls, among other things. He came to dinner one night and insisted on cooking "Italian" knowing my preference for such cuisine, and produced with almost no effort, a delicious meal that only invigorated our conversation on a wide range of topics from history to art theory to local cultural oddities. The recipe, omitting the mention of the frequent consumption of wine and the nearly nonstop laughter and conversation, went something like this (all from memory).

"It's easy," said George, describing with painterly gestures, the simple procedure of basting a chicken with generous amounts of olive oil, basil, lots of garlic and other tasty additives (such as plenty of fresh lemon, the lemon rinds crushed by hand and dropped into the pan, a few kalamata olives, generous splashes of wine and I now forget what else). It is next a simple matter of roasting the chicken in the broiler at about 452 degrees for a while or until the skin becomes crispy and the juices flow into a mix with the salt, pepper, and lemon rinds, and that's it! With a wave of his hand he said, "You just serve it with a fresh salad and some more delicious wine and VOILA! (or ecco!) and you have it, 'CHICKEN SCHMIDT'."

César Pelli

SAN MIGUEL DE TUCUMÁN, ARGENTINA
1926 - 2019

Scott Perkins

TUSA 1980

BROOKFIELD PLAZA (NEW YORK, NY) DESIGNED BY PELLI

CÉSAR PELLI was born October 12, 1926, in San Miguel de Tucumán, Argentina. His parents instilled within him a love of reading, learning, and the arts. His life in architecture began with studies at the Universidad Nacional de Tucumán, and continued at the University of Illinois at Urbana Champaign School of Architecture. In 1954, shortly after graduation, a job offer from Eero Saarinen at his practice in Bloomfield Hills, Michigan, brought César into the orbit of one of the most influential architects of his generation. The decade at Saarinen's firm, which César described as his "post-graduate experience," taught him the importance of bringing a fresh eye to each project, and a rigorous process incorporating physical models to test the reality of design concepts—techniques that César advanced throughout his career.

César originated many design concepts in his L.A. years, including circulation spines as generators and organizers of the plan; and architecture's materiality, specifically the building's skin as an expression of contemporary construction techniques.

Named Dean of the Yale School of Architecture in 1977, César opened his own practice in New Haven, Connecticut, with partners Diana Balmori and Fred Clarke. The landmark expansion and renovation of the Museum of Modern Art in New York in 1977 produced the earliest example of a design firm working with an associated firm to provide technical, contract documentation support. This method of collaboration continues to be the backbone of Pelli Clarke Pelli Architects' practice, allowing the firm to undertake global projects of any size or scale. This paradigm has had far-ranging influence on the profession at large.

- *Scott Perkins (TUSA 1980)*

RENÉE AND HENRY SEGERSTROM CONCERT HALL (COSTA MESA, CA) DESIGNED BY PELLI

César Pelli	Dinner Party

ANTIPASTO
Figs stuffed with blue cheese and Serrano Ham

PRIMO PIATTO
Rigatoni with brown butter, sage, and walnuts

SECONDO
Pork Scaloppini al Limone

INSALATA
Arugula with goat cheese, toasted nuts, and fresh fruit

DESSERT
Tarta de Santiago (Spanish almond cake) with Gelato

During my tenure with Mandarin Oriental Hotel Group, César Pelli was the design architect for a couple of our projects. We had the opportunity to enjoy meals together in Southern California and New Haven; both places we had wonderful dinners in Italian restaurants. This led me to create a menu of some contemporary Italian dishes. These courses should be enjoyed with your favorite Italian wines.

- *Scott Perkins*

Antipasto

8 BLACK MISSION OR BROWN TURKEY FIGS

2 OZ BLUE CHEESE (PREFERABLY POINT REYES OR GORGONZOLA)

4 OZ SERRANO HAM, THINLY SLICED (OR PROSCIUTTO)

Figs stuffed with blue cheese and Serrano ham

Preheat the oven to 375 degrees. Clean the figs and slice off the stem, exposing the fruit. Make a few slices 3/4 of the way through the top of each fig.

Cut slices of the blue cheese (1/8" thick) and push pieces of cheese into the slices in the fig.

Fully wrap each fig with the ham in a thin coating and place on a rimmed baking sheet.

Bake for 6 to 8 minutes until the ham is crispy and the cheese is melted.

Primo Piatto

12 OZ FRESH RIGATONI
STUFFED WITH RICOTTA
CHEESE

1 TBSP SALT

4 OZ WALNUTS (TOASTED AND
COARSELY CHOPPED)

12 OZ UNSALTED BUTTER

12 FRESH SAGE LEAVES
(LARGE - CHOPPED)

PARMEGIANO REGGIANO
(FRESHLY GRATED)

Rigatoni with Brown Butter, Sage, and Walnuts

Bring 2 quarts of water to a boil and add the salt.
Add the rigatoni and cook according to the package
instructions (generally 3-4 minutes) until al dente.

While the water is boiling, heat a medium saucepan over
medium high heat and add the butter. The butter will sputter
violently as it browns. When the butter quits bubbling (about
4 or 5 minutes) and is a medium brown color, add the walnuts and stir. Add the Sage leaves, stir, and remove from the
heat. Drain the pasta and arrange on plates. Spoon the butter
mixture on top and sprinkle liberally with the parmesan. Serve
immediately.

Secondo

FLOUR (FOR DREDGING)

1 LB PORK TENDERLOIN
SLICES (1/4" THICK /
POUNDED TO 1/8")

KOSHER SALT
BLACK PEPPER
(FRESHLY GROUND)

6 - 8 TBSP OLIVE OIL

5 OZ CHICKEN STOCK

3 OZ LEMON JUICE

3 TBSP UNSALTED BUTTER

2 TBSP FRESH BASIL
(FINELY CHOPPED)

Pork Scaloppini al Limone

Preheat the oven to 200 degrees and put a platter in to warm.
Slice the tenderloin into 1/4" thick medallions and pound them
to 1/8" thick. They should all be approximately the same size.
Season them with salt and pepper on one side.

Place a small pile of flour (for dredging the meat) into a
shallow pan near the cooktop.

Heat 2-3 TBSP of olive oil to sizzling in your largest skillet. Dip
6 pieces of meat in the flour, shake off the excess, and add the
meat to the pan. Cook as rapidly as possible – no more than 2
minutes per side until the edges are lightly browned. Transfer
the meat to the warmed serving dish in the oven.

Repeat until all the meat is cooked, adding more oil to the pan
as needed. Pour off the oil from the pan, raise the heat, and
add the chicken stock. Boil, scraping up all the brown bits from
the bottom of the pan.

Add the lemon juice, season with salt and pepper, and boil for
another minute or so.

Remove the pan from the heat, add the butter, and whisk until
blended. Stir in the basil and pour the sauce over the pork
Serve immediately.

Insalata

Arugula with goat cheese, toasted nuts, and fresh fruit

1 BUNCH FRESH ARUGULA
(WASHED, DRIED, AND STEMS
REMOVED)

3 OZ FRESH GOAT CHEESE

1 CUP WALNUTS, PECANS, OR
SLICED ALMONDS (TOASTED)

FRESH FRUIT (IN SEASON-
STRAWBERRIES, PEACHES,
BLOOD ORANGES, SATSUMAS,
PEARS)

Arrange the arugula on plates and top with large crumbles of goat cheese. Scatter the toasted nuts on top (walnuts or pecans can be broken up. Clean and slice the fruit (or section the citrus) and arrange on top. Refrigerate until ready to serve. Lightly drizzle the vinaigrette on top and serve.

Dessert

Tarta de Santiago (Spanish Almond Cake) with Gelato

1 TBSP BUTTER (FOR
GREASING THE PAN)

1 TBSP FLOUR (FOR
COATING THE PAN)

3 EXTRA LARGE EGGS

3/4 CUP WHITE SUGAR

1/2 TSP KOSHER SALT

1/4 TSP ALMOND EXTRACT

1/4 TSP VANILLA EXTRACT

1.5 CUPS ALMOND FLOUR

PINCH GROUND CINNAMON

ZEST OF 1/2 LEMON

3 TBLS DEMERARA SUGAR

1/2 CUP SLICED ALMONDS
(CHOPPED)

Heat the oven to 350 degrees with rack in the middle position. Butter the bottom and sides of a 9" cake pan and add a round piece of parchment paper. Butter the parchment. Dust with flour.

In the bowl of a stand mixer fitted with a whisk, combine the eggs, sugar, and the extracts. Whisk on high for 45 seconds. The mixture will be thick and frothy.

Combine the cinnamon, almond flour, and the lemon zest. Add to the egg mixture and whisk until just incorporated. Pour into the prepared pan, then sprinkle with the sugar and almonds.

Bake for 35 to 50 minutes until deeply browned and the crust feels firm when gently pressed with a finger. The sides should slightly shrink away from the sides of the pan.

Cool on a wire rack for 10 minutes. Run a knife around the edges of the pan, then invert onto a plate and remove the parchment. Flip the cake onto the serving plate and cool completely.

Slice the cake and place on a plate with a scoop of your favorite gelato.

RIGHT: RESIDENCE DESIGNED BY PELLI IN JACKSON HOLE, WY

TULANE CONTRIBUTOR

Scott Perkins (TUSA 1980)

My first assignment after graduation took me to Houston and introduced me to interior architecture and hospitality design. This set me on a path of project design alternating with design leadership with luxury hotel companies. The desire to return to the design world, after a segment with Ritz-Carlton, brought me to Hirsch Bedner Associates, designing luxury hotels and resorts on six continents around the globe.

My last departure from design took me to the Mandarin Oriental Hotel Group, providing an opportunity to collaborate with many leading architects and interior designers as the design editor as well as to integrate the operational overlay to produce exceptional work. Two of these projects provided the opportunity to collaborate with César Pelli and enjoy several dinners with him.

Hospitality design drew on my love of food and wine, creating a lasting relationship with many chefs who have inspired and led me on a culinary journey. Desserts are my favorite as they are a combination of technique, construction, and detail.

FAVORITE RECIPE

Aperitivo: Ginger Rum César

1 OZ MOUNT GAY BLACK
BARREL RUM

1/2 OZ PINEAPPLE JUICE

1 VANILLA BEAN

GINGER LIQUEUR* (TO TASTE)

1 JUMBO ICE CUBE
(SQUARE OR ROUND MOLDED SHAPE –
ALMOST AS LARGE AS THE GLASS)

Zest the orange and place the zest in a glass container with the vanilla bean, syrup, and brandy. Seal and shake. Let steep for 24 hours. Remove the vanilla bean and let the mixture steep for 24 more hours. Strain the mixture through a filter into a bottle or jar for storage and let the flavors blend for 24 more hours.

Pour the ingredients into an interesting glass over the large ice cube and stir. Adjust Ginger Liqueur to taste.

*GINGER LIQUEUR

2 OZ GINGER ROOT

1 VANILLA BEAN

1 CUP SUGAR

1.5 CUPS WATER

1 ORANGE

1.5 CUPS BRANDY

Ginger Liqueur (*Make 3 days in advance – or purchase a ginger liqueur*). Peel the ginger and shave it into thin slices with a mandolin. Split the vanilla bean in half (lengthwise). Bring the ginger, vanilla, sugar, and water to a boil – reduce heat to low and simmer until ginger is soft (20 minutes). Let the syrup cool.

THE RESORT AT SINGER ISLAND – RESTAURANT (DESIGNED BY SCOTT PERKINS)

THE RITZ-CARLTON, SAN JUAN – LOBBY (DESIGNED BY SCOTT PERKINS)

Ricardo Legoretta Vilchis

MEXICO CITY, MEXICO
1931 - 2011

Andrew Mayhew Hanson

TUSA 1980

CAMINO REAL POLANCO MEXICO (MEXICO CITY, MEXICO) DESIGNED BY LEGORRETA

RICARDO LEGORRETA was born in Mexico City in 1931. He studied architecture at the National Autonomous University of Mexico (UNAM) under José Villagrán García (1901-1982), the foremost proponent of the International Style in mid-20th century Mexico. After graduating in 1952, Legorreta joined Villagrán as his partner and established his own practice in 1964, completing the groundbreaking Camino Real Hotel in 1968. The firm completed corporate, public projects, and private residences during the 70's and '80's when several themes emerged: massive, brightly-colored walls with openings placed to maximize light and views, geometric volumes linked together by outdoor spaces, wide hallways, and generous spaces.

Legorreta combined many aspects of the International Style with elements derived from the climate, colors, and vernacular architecture of Mexico. Villagran and Luis Baragán both influenced Legoretta as well as painter Chucho Reyes. In an interview with David Dillon for Architectural Record about the College of Santa Fe Visual Arts Center in 2000, Legorreta commented, "modern architects want too much clarity in a building... They miss the pleasures of mystery and intrigue." Ricardo received numerous awards including the American Institute of Architects Gold Medal (2000), the AIA's highest honor, and the prestigious Praemium Imperiale by the Art Association of Japan (2011).

- Andrea Mayhew Hanson (TUSA 1980)

ZOCALO RESIDENTIAL COMPOUND (SANTA FE, NM) DESIGNED BY LEGORRETA

Ricardo Legorreta | Dinner Party

APPETIZER
Rustic Jicama with Lime and Chile*

SIDE DISH
Grilled Street Corn (Elotes)

MAIN COURSE
Cochinita Pibil Tacos

DRINK
Hibiscus Paloma

DESSERT
Mango Sorbet
Polvorones Rosas
*(Mexican Sugar Cookies)***

This menu celebrates simple, fresh Mexican street food with a rosy-hued, tequila-based cocktail. Each dish is bold in flavor and in color and reflects Legoretta's love of the simplicity of small Mexican towns and villages, unpretentious and riotous in their unexpected color.

- *Andrea Mayhew Hanson*

Grilled Street Corn (Elotes)

6-8 EARS CORN, SHUCKED

1/2 CUP MAYONNAISE

1/2 CUP SOUR CREAM

1/2 CUP CILANTRO LEAVES, MINCED, PLUS MORE FOR GARNISH

1 CLOVE GARLIC, MINCED

1/4 TSP GROUND CHIPOTLE POWDER, MORE TO TASTE

2 TSP LIME ZEST

2 TBSP FRESH LIME JUICE

1/2 CUP CRUMBLED COTIJA CHEESE

DIVIDED LIME WEDGES

Heat grill to 400 degrees. In a bowl, whisk together the sour cream, mayonnaise, cilantro, garlic, chipotle pepper, lime zest, and lime juice. Taste and season the mixture with salt if needed. Set aside.

Place the husked corn directly onto grill grates. Grill the corn for about 3 minutes, undisturbed, or until kernels begin to turn golden brown and look charred. Turn over and repeat.

When all sides are browned, remove from the grill onto a plate. Using a brush or a spoon, coat each ear of corn with the crema mixture. Sprinkle with crumbled cojita.

*Raw jicama spears tossed in fresh lime juice and sprinkled with salt and chili powder or Tajin
(Tajin Clasico Seasoning is made with a unique blend of lime, mild chili peppers, and sea salt)

Cochinita Pibil Tacos

3-4 POUNDS PORK SHOULDER OR PORKLOIN,
CUT INTO 1.5-INCH CHUNKS

1 CUP FRESHLY-SQUEEZED ORANGE JUICE

1/3 CUP FRESHLY-SQUEEZED LIME JUICE

1 (3.5 OUNCE) PACKAGE ACHIOTE PASTE

1 TSP GROUND CUMIN

1/2 CUP SLICED ONION

3-4 CLOVES OF GARLIC, MINCED

KOSHER SALT AND FRESHLY-CRACKED
BLACK PEPPER (TO TASTE)

SERVE WITH:
PICKLED RED ONIONS (SEE PAGE 169)
CILANTRO
COTIJA CHEESE
LIME WEDGES
OPTIONAL: GUACAMOLE, PICO DE GALLO

Combine the achiote paste, orange juice, lime juice and cumin and garlic in a blender or food processor. Add salt and pepper to taste. Put cubed pork in the bowl of your pressure cooker or slow cooker, pour marinade over and stir to coat. Slow cook the pork on high for 4 hours or for 8 hours on low. If using a pressure cooker cook on manual for 40 minutes, followed by a 15-minute natural release. Cook until pork is tender and shreds easily with a fork.

Combine with the remaining liquid to the consistency of your favorite pulled pork. Serve in tacos or over cilantro lime rice. Accompaniments are the same for either. Store leftover pork for a few days refrigerated.

Toast corn tortillas on the grill then fill with pork. Top with pickled onions, crumbled cotija cheese, and a sprig of cilantro and lime wedge. Serve with optional guacamole and pico de gallo (fresh salsa). Prepare two tacos for each serving with more if desired.

Hibiscus Paloma

1 GRAPEFRUIT WEDGE

2 OUNCES FRESH GRAPEFRUIT JUICE

1/2 OUNCE FRESH LIME JUICE

1 TSP HIBISCUS SIMPLE SYRUP*

2 OUNCES WHITE TEQUILA

CLUB SODA

KOSHER SALT OR TAJIN

*HIBISCUS SIMPLE SYRUP

1/2 CUP DRIED HIBISCUS FLOWERS

1 CUP WATER

1 CUP SUGAR

Pour kosher salt or Tajin onto a small plate. Rub the rim of a highball glass with a grapefruit or lime wedge and dip the rim of glass in salt. (Rimming the glass is optional.) Combine grapefruit juice, lime juice, hibiscus simple syrup, and tequila in cocktail shaker with a few ice cubes. Strain into prepared glasses and top off with a splash of club soda.

Bring water to a boil over medium-high heat in a small pot. Turn off heat, add the hibiscus flowers, and steep for 5 minutes. Strain out the hibiscus flowers. Return the pot to the stove and add the sugar. Heat on medium until the sugar dissolves. Remove from heat and allow to cool before using. Store in a glass container.

**Purchase Mango Sorbet from your favorite ice cream shop
and Polvorones Rosas from your local panaderia.

TULANE CONTRIBUTOR

Andrea Mayhew Hanson (TUSA 1980)

My career has taken me from NOLA to San Francisco and back to my native New Mexico. As a partner at Dekker/Perich/Sabatini, I led our Interior Design practice across all of our offices and in the last year moved into my role as Principal of Workplace Strategy. In addition to designing interiors for healthcare, corporate, and higher education facilities, I have a special passion for workplace performance and designs that promote wellbeing in all industries. As a WELL AP, my goal is to apply evidenced-based strategies to create healthy places for people to work and thrive.

Favorite projects include corporate workspace projects for The Gap, Netflix, Vanguard, ConocoPhillips, DaVita Healthcare and the Thornburg Companies in collaboration with Legoretta + Legoretta. Ricardo spoke at the opening of the Thornburg Campus about the small towns throughout Mexico that influenced his work through the simple forms and juxtaposition of unlikely colors, the "irresponsible use of color." A lesson in unexpected delight.

FAVORITE RECIPE

Basilisk Cocktail

MUDDLE LIGHTLY TOGETHER:

1 OZ LEMON JUICE

1 OZ SIMPLE SYRUP

4 BASIL LEAVES

Add 2 oz Bourbon (Basil Haydon is my personal favorite). Shake with ice. Strain into a chilled glass or over rocks in a highball glass and top with a splash of soda water.

UNEXPECTED DELIGHT:
TINKERING AND TRAVELING IN DAISY
SOUTH DAKOTA SEPTEMBER 2020

IMAGE ON RIGHT COURTESTY OF ANDREA MAYHEW HANSON

Harry Wolf

CHARLOTTE, NORTH CAROLINA
1935 -

Chris Knight

TUSA 1971

"STRENGTH, UTILITY AND BEAUTY"
- Vitruvius

HARRY WOLF was born in Charlotte, North Carolina, and graduated in 1958 with a BS in Architecture from Georgia Tech followed by a Bachelor of Architecture from MIT in 1960. After working for a few firms including Odell Associates and Graves and Toy, he founded Wolf Associates Architects in 1966 in Charlotte, North Carolina. There he led a small studio of highly dedicated young architects who ascribed to Wolf's vision of creating world-class modernist architecture. Wolf closed that office in 1983 and moved to New York where he taught at Harvard and Columbia, then moved to Los Angles in 1988. Harry Wolf was, from the beginning, an unrelenting and unapologic modernist. His designs are continuously recognized for their consistently powerful presence while maintaining an elegant resolution of aesthetic and purpose. Wolf's acute attention to detail, respect for materials and application, and commitment to refinement and simplification result in works of inherent beauty.

Projects of note are: Nations Bank Florida Headquarters, Tampa, Florida; Mecklenburg County Courthouse, Charlotte, North Carolina; School Of Design Addition at North Carolina State University, Raleigh, North Carolina; and UNCC Administrative Building, Charlotte, North Carolina.

Wolf has won 30+ awards from the national AIA, including their national Honor Award five times. He now lives in Porto, Portugal.

- Chris Knight (TUSA 1971)

LEFT AND ABOVE: NCNB NATIONAL BANK (TAMPA, FL) DESIGNED BY HARRY WOLF

| Harry Wolf | Vitruvius's Delight (Breakfast)* |

MAIN COURSE
Waffles with Vanilla
Cream Sauce

DRINK
Mimosas

To be served as breakfast entrée at the end of the charrette

Waffles with Vanilla Cream Sauce

1 CUP ALL-PURPOSE FLOUR

2 TBSP SUGAR

1 TSP BAKING POWDER

1/4 TSP SALT

1 CUP MILK

2 LARGE EGGS

1/2 STICK UNSALTED BUTTER, MELTED

In a large bowl, whisk flour, sugar, baking powder, and salt. Set aside. In a small bowl, whisk milk and eggs. Pour over flour mixture and whisk gently to combine. Gently whisk in butter. Place mixture in a waffle iron and cook 2 to 3 minutes until the color of Cordoba Shell Limestone at sunset.

VANILLA CREAM SAUCE

2 CUPS WHIPPING CREAM

1 CUP SUGAR

2 TBSP ALL-PURPOSE FLOUR

1/2 CUP BUTTER

1 TSP VANILLA EXTRACT

1 RASPBERRY

Stir first three ingredients together in a saucepan. Add butter and cook, stirring constantly, over medium heat until butter is melted and mixture begins to boil. Cook, stirring constantly, 3 minutes or until mixture is slightly thickened. Remove from heat and stir in vanilla. Dredge waffle in the vanilla cream and serve warm on a 10-inch square black plate. Set plate centered on a 20-inch square white placemat. Add raspberry to center of waffle. Serve with a very dry champagne.

Mimosas

3/4 CUP CHAMPAGNE, CHILLED

1/4 CUP FRESH SQUEEZED ORANGE JUICE

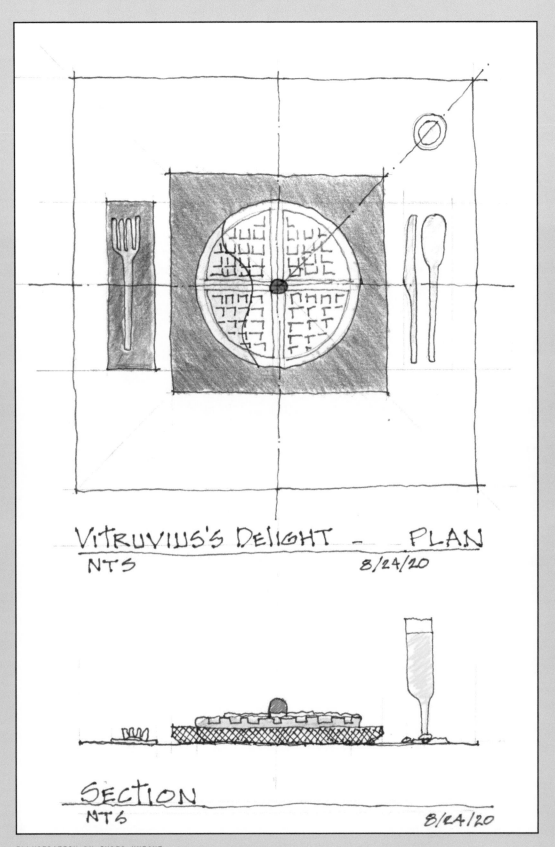

VITRUVIUS'S DELIGHT — PLAN
NTS   8/24/20

SECTION
NTS   8/24/20

ILLUSTRATION BY CHRIS KNIGHT

TULANE CONTRIBUTOR

Chris Knight (TUSA 1971)

Chris Knight first meet John Lawrence in 1966 as a freshman at Tulane School of Architecture. After a 40+ year career as a practicing architect, Chris retired to Fairhope, Alabama, where he spends his time as a landscape painter. You can reach Chris at knightatthebay@gmail.com

FAVORITE RECIPE

Grilled Pork Chops with Peaches

1 TBSP ORANGE ZEST, GRATED

1 TSP FENNEL SEEDS, CRUSHED

1 TSP DRIED ROSEMARY

1 TSP OLIVE OIL

1 TSP SALT

1 TSP PEPPER

2 6-OZ PORK CHOPS, BONE-IN, 3/4" THICK

4 PEACHES

Preheat grill to medium high heat. Prepare herb rub by mixing together first 6 ingredients in a small cup until mixture forms a paste. Rub pork chops with mixture. Place chops on grill and grill until pork chops are done, about 5 minutes per side.

Cut peaches in half and place on grill cut side down. Grill until tender, about 5 minutes. Place peaches on grill when you turn the pork chops, and everything will be done at the same time.

RIGHT: WEEKS CREEK (2018), PAINTING BY CHRIS KNIGHT

Stephen
Jacobs

NEW YORK, NEW YORK
1942 - 2014

Geoffrey Butler

TUSA 1980

THE STEVE JACOBS HOUSE, EXTERIOR AND INTERIOR (NEW ORLEANS, LA)

Born in New York City in 1942, Steve received his Bachelor of Architecture from M.I.T. and his Masters of Architecture from the University of Pennsylvania, where he studied with Louis I. Kahn. Steve began teaching design as a Peace Corps volunteer in Bolivia, then went on to teach and lecture in Colombia, Argentina, and Mexico, as well as practice architecture in New York and New Orleans. Steve moved to New Orleans in 1971 and had a long and respected career at the School of Architecture as teacher, administrator, author, mentor, and friend.

Steve had a deep love for Bolivia, and following his retirement from Tulane, pursued his Ph.D at the Stone Center, conducting original research on the guilds and artisan communities in colonial Sucre, Bolivia. He was part of the original team that presented the first conference of the Bolivian Studies Association. Steve's interests were encyclopedic and enthusiastic, ranging from computers to music, literature, architecture, food, and history. His distinctive home and studio in New Orleans, which he designed, now serves as a residence for visiting faculty members and a venue for school functions.

- Geoffrey Butler (TUSA 1980)

Faculty Fall 1981: down; Rodreguez, Mouton, Heard, Oppenheimer, Helmer, Barron, Culvahouse, Filson, Young; up; Goodwin, Cizek, Denton, Jacobs, Shapiro, Rock, Ubbelohde, Calongne.

Professor Stephen Jacobs, mid 1980's.

Stephen Jacobs	Dinner Party

MAIN COURSE
Jambalaya

DESSERT
Caramel Cup Custard

SIDE DISH
Rich Corn Bread

It was the fall of 1974, and a young professor was instructing me on the finer points of a coffee wash on a figure ground of the Hagia Sophia; that's when Steve and I started a life-long friendship. Steve Jacobs was instrumental in introducing me to everything New Orleans, especially the neighborhood food and beverages, but of course there was Mardi Gras and Jazz Fest, too. I think it's safe to say that Paul Prudhomme, Emeril Lagasse, and Brennan's represented the simple traditional food and drink of New Orleans that Steve was such a fan of. To truly get the essence of Steve, I suggest you queue up Kermit Ruffins, Ellis Marsalis, Verdi, Tchaikovsky, Dr. John, Professor Long Hair, or even a little gospel music, open an Abita Amber, and start cooking. While you're waiting for the shrimp to boil and the corn bread to brown, curl up with your cats (or dogs) and enjoy the music and your fondest memories of Steve. I fondly reminisce about savoring a muffuletta, sipping a cold beer, and listening to a local saxophonist at the Napoleon House with Steve.

- *Geoffrey Butler*

Rich Corn Bread

1 CUP YELLOW CORN MEAL

1 CUP FLOUR

4 TBSP FINE BAKING POWDER

1 TSP BAKING SODA

2 TSP CREAM OF TARTAR

1 EAR FRESH CORN, KERNELS CUT

OFF COBB (I OFTEN SUBSTITUTE 1/4 CUP GRITS)

3/4 TSP SALT

1 CUP SOUR CREAM (YOGURT WORKS TOO)

1/4 CUP MILK

2 EGGS, WELL BEATEN

4 TBSP MELTED BUTTER

Preheat oven to 425°F. Combine the cornmeal, flour, sugar, baking soda, cream of tartar and salt, mix well. Quickly add the sour cream, milk, eggs and melted butter. Stir just to mix. Fold in the fresh corn. Spoon into pan and bake about 20 minutes (until toothpick comes out clean). Cool and cut into squares. Serve with sweet butter and honey.
Recipe from Arlene Evans, who grew up in Abita Springs. Her husband Hayden graduated from Tulane Medical School. We've been good buddies for over 25 years.

Caramel Cup Custard

1 1/4 CUP SUGAR

1 TBSP LEMON JUICE

3 EGGS

1 CUP HEAVY CREAM

3/4 TEASPOON VANILLA EXTRACT

Preheat oven to 350. Combine 1 cup sugar and the lemon juice in a heavy, nonreactive saucepan over medium heat. Cook, stirring constantly, for about 10 minutes, or until sugar dissolves and turns smooth and brown. Remove from heat. Spoon 1 tablespoon of the mixture into four 6-ounce custard cups.

Combine eggs, cream, vanilla, and the remaining 1/4 cup sugar in a small mixing bowl. Whisk to dissolve the sugar. Evenly divide the mixture among the custard cups. Place the cups in a baking pan large enough to hold them comfortably. Fill the pan with enough water to reach three quarters of the way up the side of the cups.

Bake for about an hour, or until the custard sets and a knife inserted in the custard comes out clean. Let cool, then refrigerate for at least 4 hours. When ready to serve, use a thin knife to loosen the custard around the edges of the cup. Invert onto chilled dessert plates.

Recipe from Louisiana Real & Rustic 1996 by Emeril Lagasse

Jambalaya

1 TSP SALT

1 TSP WHITE PEPPER

1 TSP DRY MUSTARD

1 TSP CAYENNE PEPPER

1 TSP FILE POWDER

1/2 TSP GROUND CUMIN

1/2 TSP GROUND BLACK PEPPER

1/2 TSP DRIED THYME

4 TBSP MARGARINE

6 OZ TASSO HAM

6 OZ ANDOUILLE SAUSAGE

1 1/2 CUP CHOPPED ONIONS

1 1/2 CUP CHOPPED CELERY

1 CUP CHOPPED GREEN PEPPER

1 1/2 TSP MINCED GARLIC

2 CUPS UNCOOKED RICE

4 CUPS CHICKEN STOCK

Combine the seasoning mix ingredients in a small bowl. Set aside. In a large heavy skillet, melt the margarine over high heat. Add the meats and cook for 5 minutes, or until browned. Add the onions, celery, peppers, seaosning mix, and garlic. Stir well and continue cooking until browned, about 10 to 12 minutes, stirring occasionally and scraping the pan bottom well. Stir in the rice and cook 5 minutes, stirring and scraping pan bottom occasionally. Add stock, stirring well. Bring mixture to a boil; reduce heat and simmer until rice is tender but still a bit crunchy, about 20 minutes, stirring occasionally toward the end of cooking time.

Adapted from Paul Prudhomme's Louisiana Kitchen.

TULANE CONTRIBUTOR

Geoffrey Butler (TUSA 1980)

I arrived at Tulane, sight unseen, in the Fall of 1974 after graduating from Deerfield Academy. I made a valiant effort to swim for Tulane my freshman year, but soon decided that sneaking out of the design studio two hours early every day for swim practice was not a long-term option. I worked a few summers in New Orleans for the harbor tugboat company E.N. Bisso & Sons, located at the foot of Audubon Park. Following graduation, I moved to Phillipsburg, Montana, where I worked for the B-H Ranch, initially irrigating fields and eventually herding cattle; it was a wonderful year. Having been offered a job with Global Marin Drilling Co. on the West Coast, I hopped on a bus to Goleta, California, and started a three week on, three week off year-long stint as a roustabout and roughneck. (I still have all my fingers.) In 1982, Bill Morrish invited me to work for his fledging firm, City West, in San Francisco. I also worked for Robinson Mills and Williams, William Turnbull Associates, Hewlett Packard as campus Architect, and started the partnership Richardson-Butler in 1986. Since 1991 I have been a sole practitioner. In 1984 I married my beautiful wife Fabia and have three adult children, Natalie, Brad, and Reese. I am grateful to have lived in Mill Valley, California, for more than 30 years, given the incredible access to water and open space. Four years ago I fulfilled a wish for my 60th birthday and swam the length of Lake Tahoe, 21.3 miles, sans wetsuit.

LEED PLATINUM HOME DESIGNED BY GEOFFREY BUTLER (MILL VALLEY, CA)

Chicken Pot Pie

SEASONING MIX

1 TBSP SALT

1 TSP WHITE PEPPER

1 TSP PAPRIKA

1 TSP GARLIC POWDER

3/4 TSP ONION POWDER

3/4 TSP DRY MUSTARD

3/4 TSP DRIED THYME LEAVES

1/2 TSP GROUND CARDAMOM

1/2 TSP BLACK PEPPER

1/2 TSP GROUND SAVORY

DOUGH

2 CUPS ALL-PURPOSE FLOWER

3/4 CUP TOASTED CORNMEAL
(SEE NOTE P.168)

1 TBSP SEASONING MIX (SEE ABOVE)

1/2 LB (2 STICKS) UNSALTED BUTTER,
CUT INTO PATS

1/2 CUP CHILLED CHICKEN STOCK

FILLING

2 TBSP + 3/4 TSP SEASONING MIX

2 LBS BONELESS SKINLESS CHICKEN BREASTS

8 SLICES BACON, DICED

2 CUPS CHOPPED ONIONS

1 CUP CHOPPED GREEN BELL PEPPERS

1 1/2 CUPS CHOPPED CELERY

1 CUP FRESH CORN KERNELS (ABOUT 2 EARS)

4 CUPS CHICKEN STOCK

3 CLOVES

1/4 CUP TOASTED CORNMEAL

1 CUP TINY PEARL ONIONS, PEELED

3 TBSP CHOPPED FRESH PARSLEY

2 CUPS SLICED CARROTS

FINISH

ALL-PURPOSE FLOUR

VEGETABLE OIL COOKING SPRAY

Combine the seasoning mix ingredients thoroughly in a small bowl. FOR THE DOUGH, combine the flour, toasted cornmeal, and seasoning mix in the bowl of a food processor and pulse until blended, about 5 or 6 times. Distribute the butter over the dry ingredients and process until blended, 25 to 30 seconds. With the machine running, add the chilled stock in a thin stream, and process until thoroughly blended, about 40 seconds. Form the dough into a ball and refrigerate for at least 30 minutes. FOR THE FILLING, sprinkle 1 tablespoon of the seasoning mix all over the chicken and pat it in well with your hands.

Place the bacon in a 12-inch skillet and fry over high heat until crisp and brown, about 8 to 9 minutes. Remove the bacon from the skillet with a slotted spoon and drain on paper towels. Heat the bacon fat remaining in the skillet over high heat, add the chicken, and fry, turning several times, until lightly browned, about 7 to 10 minutes. Remove the chicken to a bowl.

Add the chopped onions, bell peppers, celery, corn, and 1 tablespoon of the seasoning mix to the fat in the skillet. Cook, scraping the bottom of the skillet occasionally as the mixture forms crusts, about 5 minutes. Pour any chicken juices that have accumulated in the bowl plus 1/2 cup of the stock into the skillet and scrape up any crust on the bottom. Add the cloves and simmer until the mixture begins to stick again, about 6 minutes. Add another 1/2 cup stock, scrape the bottom of the skillet, and simmer until most of the liquid has evaporated, about 6 to 8 minutes. Stir in the toasted cornmeal and cook...

(Continued on Page 168)

Malcolm Heard

COLUMBUS, MISSISSIPPI
1943 - 2001

Tim Culvahouse

TUSA 1979

LOFTIN HOUSE DESIGNED BY MALCOLM HEARD (MOUNT PLEASANT, MS)

In the spring of 1978, MALCOLM HEARD taught the studio that, for me, did the most to put New Orleans in perspective and to put architecture into a larger cultural context. He gave three assignments. The first was to plan a menu and design a space in which to serve it. The second asked us to design the house portrayed in Edward Hopper's "Rooms by the Sea." Over spring break, we read Walker Percy's *The Moviegoer* and returned to campus eager to design a gas station. ("Evening is the best time in Gentilly. There are not so many trees and the buildings are low and the world is all sky . . . . Most of the commercial buildings are empty except the filling stations where attendants hose down the concrete under the glowing discs and shells and stars.") Mac, however, asked us to design a new Prytania Theatre—not a bad alternative. Mac's *French Quarter Manual: An Architectural Guide to New Orleans' Vieux Carré* is a lucid account of type and style as they relate to the evolving culture of the French Quarter. Its insights reach deeper than the physical fabric that it describes. "Myths," he writes, "intensify themselves. Because courtyards have been described as tropical or jungle-like, people plant more banana trees and palms."

Mac's most well-known building is the Lafayette Archway at the Piazza d'Italia — a study in abstraction, material transformation, and forced perspective, done while he was at Perez. Later, from the mid-1990s until his death in 2001, he collaborated on a number of mostly residential projects, such as the Loftin House in Mount Pleasant, Mississippi, with fellow Tulane faculty member Scott Bernard. It was in his own, lovingly restored Creole cottage on Louisa Street in the Bywater that I enjoyed his Old Fashioned.

- *Tim Culvahouse (TUSA 1979)*

LEFT: COVER OF *FRENCH QUARTER MANUAL: AN ARCHITECTURAL GUIDE TO NEW ORLEANS' VIEUX CARRÉ*
RIGHT: HEARD'S RESTORED CREOLE COTTAGE, LOUISA STREET, BYWATER NEIGHBORHOOD (NEW ORLEANS, LA)

| Malcolm Heard | Signature Recipes |

MAIN COURSE
Tomato Soup

DRINK
Mac Heard's Old Fashioned

Tomato Soup

As related by Alicia Rogan Heard:

"Mac and I made this tomato soup just one time, but it remained his favorite. It is based on the recipe for tomato soup in the *Times Picayune Creole Cookbook* of 1966."

2 QUARTS OF PURE TOMATO JUICE	4 CLOVES
A GILL OF RICE	A SPRIG OF THYME
3 ONIONS	A PINCH OF SUGAR TO TASTE
8 ALLSPICE	PEPPER AND SALT

Stew the tomatoes for about 2 hours, and then extract the juice. Add the other ingredients and boil for about an hour and a half; then strain. The rice, being creamy, should now make the soup as thick as cream. Serve with croutons or quenelles.

"The first day we gathered all the Creole tomatoes we could find at Langenstein's and returned on our bikes to begin boiling and straining. We discovered that it takes many tomatoes to make two quarts of juice, so we biked to Langenstein's the second day to gather more. We learned what a gill was and used purple onions instead of yellow ones. We added more thyme than one sprig and probably fresh parsley finely chopped. We used a mortar and pestle to crush the tomatoes and a colander to strain the juices. The third day we cooked the soup gently over a low flame, stirring and tasting and allowing it to rest from time to time. By the end of the day, it had reached a good consistency and a beautiful color. Our efforts made two small bowls. We had it for supper that night with hot French bread and butter."

- Alicia Rogan Heard

Mac Heard's Old Fashioned

Muddle 1/2 tsp. sugar (or more, to taste), 1 tsp. Maraschino cherry juice, a tiny bit of water, and one or two drops of lemon juice in an Old Fashioned glass. Add ice cubes, one and a half or two jiggers of Jack Daniel's Green Label, and seven or eight dashes of Peychaud's bitters. Give it all one quick swirl with a spoon, and rub a slice of lemon quickly around the rim. Decorate with a twist of lemon peel, a cherry, and an orange slice, or, better, a kumquat fresh or preserved.

Tim Culvahouse (TUSA 1979)

Tim Culvahouse, FAIA, is a professional development and editorial consultant for architecture and related disciplines. He is the editor of *arcCA DIGEST*, the quarterly journal of the AIA California Council; editor of *The Tennessee Valley Authority: Design & Persuasion* (2007); and editor and contributing author, with Ellen Lou, of John Lund Kriken's *Building Saigon South: Sustainable Lessons for a Livable Future* (2017). He has written for a wide range of journals, including a series on the architecture and urbanism of New Orleans in *Places*. Tim was formerly Head of the Department of Architecture at Rhode Island School of Design and Associate Dean for Design & Architectural Studies at California College of the Arts, and he has held visiting professorships at UC Berkeley, Carleton University (Ottawa), and Tulane School of Architecture. From 2008 to 2010, he was chair of the board of Public Architecture.

The Creole Contentment

1.5 OZ. COGNAC

1.0 OZ. MADEIRA (VERDELHO OR RAINWATER, RATHER THAN THE SWEETER BUAL OR MALVASIA)

1 TSP. MARASCHINO LIQUEUR

3-4 DASHES OF ORANGE BITTERS

In *The Gentleman's Companion: Being an Exotic Drinking Book, or, Around the World with Jigger, Beaker and Flask* (1939), Charles H. Baker, Jr. describes the Creole Contentment as "an Insidious Pleasantry from that Charming Hot-Bed of Intrigue & Culture which Is the Pulse of the Great Delta Country—New Orleans." Like many cocktails of the era, it is too sweet. With adjustments (the original calls for equal parts cognac, Madeira, and maraschino), it is made like this, stirred with ice.

RIGHT: ILLUSTRATION BY TIM CULVAHOUSE

Katie's Linguini with Clam Sauce

16 OZ. PACKAGE LINGUINI, COOKED PER PACKAGE DIRECTIONS

3 TBSP MINCED GARLIC

1 CUP CHOPPED PARSLEY, TIGHTLY PACKED

3 6.5-OZ CANS MINCED CLAMS, WITH LIQUID

4 TBSP OLIVE OIL

3/4 CUP DRY WHITE WINE

1 TSP DRIED OREGANO

RED PEPPER FLAKES, TO TASTE

In a sauté pan large enough to eventually hold the linguini, cook the garlic in the olive oil until golden. Add the wine and the liquid from the clams. Add oregano and a good shake of red pepper flakes. Bring to a boil, then reduce to simmer and cook until reduced by 1/3. Add the clams, followed a minute later by the chopped parsley. Fold the cooked linguini into the sauce. Salt and pepper to taste. Serve with grated parmesan cheese.

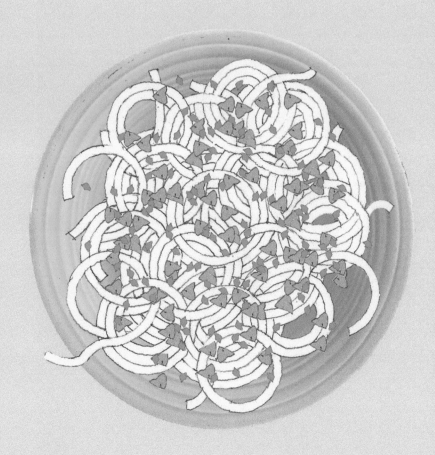

Alberto
Campo Baeza

VALLADOLID, SPAIN
1946 -

Lynn Scott Paden

TUSA 1981

MUSEO DE LA MEMORIA DE ANDALUCÍA (ANDALUSIA'S MUSEUM OF MEMORY) (GRANADA, SPAIN) DESIGNED BY BAEZA

ALBERTO CAMPO BAEZA was born in Valladolid, Spain, in the province of Castilla y Leon. When he was two, his family moved to the port city of Cádiz in Andalucía, where his grandfather was an architect. The ancient city and the quality of its light inspired Alberto from his earliest years. He believes in architecture as a Built Idea with the principle components being Gravity, that constructs space, and Light, that constructs time.

A tenured professor at the Escuela Técnica Superior de Arquitectura de Madrid (ETSAM), where he has taught for half a century, he has also been an invited lecturer and professor at the Eidgenössische Technische Hochschule in Zurich, the École Polytechnique Fédérale in Lausanne, the University of Pennsylvania, Kansas State University, the Catholic University of America, L'Ecole d'Architecture in Belgium, the Technische Universität in Austria, as well as our own Tulane School of Architecture alongside Professor Errol Barron.

His works have been widely celebrated: from the early houses of Casa Turégano, Casa de Blas, and Casa Gaspar to his larger later works of the Fundació Balears d'Innovació i Tecnologia in Mallorca, the Caja Granada Fundación, and the Museo Memoria de Andalucía both in Granada.

Campo Baeza's works are immediately recognizable for their purity of form and clarity of composition across all scales and typologies. It is his long-held belief that until an idea is constructed, it cannot be considered a work of architecture, nor the author an architect.

- Lynn Scott Paden (TUSA 1981)

"ENTRE CATEDRALES" (CÁDIZ, SPAIN) DESIGNED BY BAEZA

Alberto Campo Baeza | Dinner Party

APPETIZER
Sopa de Gato

DRINK
Cadiz Collins

MAIN COURSE
Pollo a la Canilla

ILLUSTRATION BY LYNN SCOTT PADEN

Pollo a la Canilla

The name 'a la canilla' seems to originate from the faucet that comes attached to the vat or barrel of wine. In this case Xerez, or as we know it, Sherry, is the key ingredient.

2 LBS OF CHICKEN
(LEG, THIGH AND BREAST)
CUT INTO MEDIUM PIECES

1 HEAD OF GARLIC

2 GUINDILLAS
(SMALL RED DRIED PEPPERS)

1/2 BOTTLE OF AMONTILLADO
SHERRY FROM JEREZ

SALT & PEPPER TO TASTE

Combine the chicken, salt, pepper, and diced guindillas in a bowl or pan. Cover with the sherry and refrigerate for 24 hours. The next day, remove and pat dry the chicken, save the garlic cloves, and discard the peppers and sherry.

Heat oven to 275F. In a heavy pan, introduce the olive oil and garlic, heat until garlic begins to brown, remove and set aside

Fry chicken until golden, transfer to oven until all pieces are cooked. Drain on paper towels, transfer to a warm platter, distribute garlic over top and serve.

Cádiz Collins

1 ORANGE WHEEL

3 DASHES OF WHISKY BARREL-
AGED BITTERS

2 OZ. GIN

3/4 OZ. OF AMONTILLADO SHERRY

1/2 OZ. LEMON JUICE

1/2 OZ. DEMERARA SYRUP

CLUB SODA

Combine all but orange wheel in a cocktail shaker with ice, shake well, let stand for 1 minute and serve in a tall glass. Garnish with orange wheel

Sopa de Gato

In the 16th century, the port of Cádiz was inundated by pirates whose looting and raids besieged the city. Sopa de Gato was created out of necessity to combat the ensuing hunger caused by shortages. Originally composed of water, garlic, olive oil, stale bread, and salt and pepper, today's versions often add egg and jamon. In respect for the purity Campo Baeza infuses into his creations, here is the unadulterated original reciepe.

1 LITER OF WATER

1/2 DAY OLD BAGUETTE

3/4 CUP OLIVE OIL

4 CLOVES OF GARLIC

SALT & PEPPER TO TASTE

Break baguette into chestnut size pieces, set aside. Peel, de-stem, and slice garlic. In a pan, gently fry the garlic (do not brown) in the olive oil. Heat water to a boil, add garlic and oil, reduce to a simmer. Turn off heat, add bread, cover and rest for 3 minutes. Salt and pepper to taste.

Lynn Scott Paden (TUSA 1981)

Upon graduating from TUSA I headed north, back to Pennsylvania, and then found my way to Italy and a job with Ignazio Gardella, Aldo Rossi, and Fabio Reinhart on the Teatro Carlo Felice competition. Before returning to New Orleans, I was fortunate to work in the studio of preservation architect Cesare Fera in Genova's Centro Storico. Following a brief spell with Barron & Toups, Pennsylvania called once again where Gemma de la Fuente and I opened our first studio in Lancaster, my hometown. While completing her degree at the University of Pennsylvania, Gemma invited Alberto Campo Baeza to lecture at the GSFA. To give Alberto a memorable five-star architectural tour of Philadelphia, we headed first to Frank Furness' Pennsylvania Academy of Fine Arts. An illegal left off of Broad St. had us abruptly stopped by two of Philly's finest, guns drawn. A fitting welcome to the City of Brotherly Love, and one that Alberto has never forgotten.

When the bottom dropped out in 2008, we closed our office of 25 years and moved to Washington, DC. Over the last decade, we have established a practice solely dedicated to preservation and have had the good fortune to work on more than thirty of our federal government's finest historic structures. At the President's Guest House (Blair House), we have directed projects for over a decade, working on spaces where the world's political elite have decided the course of world events. Our firm is now serving as the architects for the U.S. Treasury, caring for the works of Robert Mills, Alfred Mullett, and Cass Gilbert.

There is a deep satisfaction that comes from preserving structures by the architects that helped define L'Enfant's District, or as locals refer to it, Paris on the Potomac. Our project pictured here is not from Washington, but rather from Lancaster County, where we still occasionally take on projects. It is the adaptive reuse of a sandstone stable from 1759. The picture shows the glazed connecting corridor to the service extension which supports the stable as an events venue. The site, an iron furnace, supplied Washington with canons and shot, housed captured Hessian soldiers, and represents one of the finest intact colonial industrial sites in the country. Our passion to help perpetuate the rich history of our country, one site at a time, was kindled in Richardson Memorial by the memorable and talented professors at Tulane, the smell of night blooming jasmine walking up St. Charles at three in the morning, and hearty bowls of Red Beans and Rice on Mondays. Savor your time in this great city, there is nothing quite like it.

HORSE STABLE, ELIZABETH FURNACE, LITITZ, PA

ADAPTIVE REUSE DESIGNED BY LYNN SCOTT PADEN

Pisto Manchego a la Lancaster

3 MEDIUM ZUCCHINI (PARTED LENGTHWISE THEN CUT INTO 1" PIECES +/-)

3 MEDIUM YELLOW SQUASH (PARTED LENGTH-WISE THEN CUT INTO 1" PIECES +/-)

1 LARGE ONION (ROUGHLY CUT INTO PIECES)

2 LARGE CLOVES OF GARLIC (PEELED, HALVED, THEN SLICED)

2 TBSP BREWER'S YEAST FLAKES (TO ADD FLAVOR BOOST WITHOUT SALT)

2 CANS (28 OZ.) MARZANO WHOLE PEELED TOMATOES (OR PEELED EQUIVALENT FRESH SUMMER TOMATOES)

1 TBSP ONION POWDER

1 TBSP GARLIC POWDER

1 TSP KOSHER SALT

2 TBSP OLIVE OIL

1 EGG, BEATEN, PER SERVING

In a stock pot, add the olive oil put on medium high, add onions and salt, render down, add garlic, and do not brown, about 5-10 minutes. Add zucchini and squash, toss with onions and garlic, cover, cook on medium-low for 20 minutes, occasionally turning gently.

Add the tomatoes and then cut in half with kitchen shears. Mix well, cover and cook on low side of medium for 30 minutes. Uncover, stir gently, and cook another 30 minutes on simmer. Stir occasionally, allowing to reduce down and thicken.

Warm soup bowls in the oven at 170F and when ready, bring the pisto to just below a boil, add to bowl and stir in 1/2 to 1 beaten egg per serving. Allow egg to disperse and thicken as in egg drop soup.

Serve with a summer rosé, a Rioja Crianza or a crisp light beer. Some Spaniards drizzle some olive oil on top at the table. Crusty bread to soak up the balance is a must.

Santiago Calatrava

BENIMÀMET, SPAIN
1951 -

John Wallace

TUSA 1981

MILWUAKEE ART MUSEUM (MILWAUKEE, MN) DESIGNED BY SANTIAGO CALATRAVA

SANTIAGO CALATRAVA VALLS was born in 1951, in Benimàmet, Spain (now part of Valencia). As a child, Calatrava had an interest in the arts and took drawing and painting classes at the age of eight. In his teens, he was an exchange student with a family in Paris and visited Switzerland before returning to Valencia to finish high school. After completing his secondary education, Calatrava enrolled and received his diploma in Architecture from the Polytechnic University of Valencia in 1974. He later enrolled in the Swiss Federal Institute of Technology in Zürich, Switzerland, receiving a second degree in civil engineering in 1979. Calatrava was influenced by the work of the Swiss engineer Robert Maillart which taught him that, "with an adequate combination of force and mass, you can create emotion."

While in school in Zürich, he helped a veterinary student complete some drawings for a project, and as thanks, the student gave him the skeleton of a dog. The skeleton hangs in Calatrava's office and is considered to be an inspiration for much of his work. These curving spines, usually of poured concrete but still delicate-looking, became a hallmark of Calatrava's style.

As a structural engineer, Calatrava was fascinated by bridges and began taking on these projects. Eventually, he would complete almost 50 spans around the world. Calatrava's suspension bridges are often made from white concrete and steel cables. By redefining the standards of symmetry, he introduced highly sculptural and organic solutions.

- *John Wallace (TUSA 1981)*

THE OCULUS (NEW YORK, NY) DESIGNED BY SANTIAGO CALATRAVA

| Santiago Calatrava | Dinner Party |

MAIN COURSE
Crabmeat Paella with Peas

DRINK
Porto Tonico

CALATRAVA TABLE SETTING (DESIGNED, BUILT, AND PHOTOGRAPHED BY JOHN WALLACE)
THE SAMUEL BECKETT BRIDGE (DUBLIN, IRELAND) DESIGNED BY SANTIAGO CALATRAVA

Porto Tonico

There is a complicated relationship between Spain and Portugal. Some have described it as a sibling rivalry. That aside, I believe that Santiago would find the following Portuguese recipe very refreshing as he prepares his favorite Paella on a hot summer's evening. White port can be hard to find, but it's worth it.

1 PART WHITE PORT
2 PARTS TONIC
HEALTHY SLICE OF ORANGE
FRESH MINT (OPTIONAL)
ICE

Select an appropriately-sized vessel. Add ice, then pour in the white port and tonic. Introduce a gentle squeeze of orange slice into the drink. Stir. Add mint if you feel like it.

Crabmeat Paella with Peas

Spain's third largest city, Valencia, is located on the coast of the Mediterranean. Established as a Roman military outpost circa 130 B.C., it was fought for over the millennium. The Moors gained control of the area in the 700's and introduced rice and saffron to the region. With access to rice (from the south), saffron (from the west), and seafood from the Mediterranean, an extraordinary dish was created: Paella.

My association of paella with Santiago Calatrava is straightforward. It would be a comfort food to many Spaniards who would find themselves far from home. I've selected a Crabmeat with Peas recipe based on the availability of ingredients and ease of preparation.

8 CLOVES FRESH GARLIC, MINCED

4 TBSP FRESH PARSLEY, MINCED

1 TBSP FRESH THYME LEAVES

1/2 TSP CRUSHED RED PEPPER

1 BAY LEAF (MEDITERRANEAN)

SEA SALT

6 OZ CAN FLAKED CRABMEAT (THIS IS FOR THE BROTH)

1/4 TSP SAFFRON THREAD, CRUMBLED

5 3/4 CUPS CLAM JUICE OR FISH BROTH

8 TBSP OLIVE OIL

1 MEDIUM ONION, FINELY CHOPPED

6 TBSP LEEKS (WHITE PARTS ONLY), MINCED

2 SMALL GREEN ITALIAN PEPPERS OR 1 MEDIUM BELL PEPPER

2 MEDIUM TOMATOES (SKINNED, SEEDED, AND FINELY CHOPPED)

1/2 CUP CARROT (COOKED, THEN FINELY CHOPPED)

1/4 CUP BRANDY

1/2 TSP SMOKED PAPRIKA

3 CUPS SHORT GRAIN RICE

2 TBSP FRESH LEMON JUICE

1 CUP FROZEN PEAS

1 LB LUMP CRAB MEAT

Mash four cloves of garlic into a paste using a mortar. Add the parsley, thyme, crushed red pepper, bay leaf and 1/4 tsp. salt, then mash all ingredients as well. Drain liquid from crabmeat and combine in a pot with the saffron and enough broth to make six cups of liquid. Preheat oven to 400 degrees.

Using an 18" paella pan (or shallow casserole), heat the oil. Add the onion, leeks, peppers, and remaining four cloves of garlic and sauté slowly until the vegetables soften. Stir in cooked carrots and brandy, then bring to a boil until the liquid evaporates. Stir in paprika and rice and coat well. Add all of the broth and lemon juice and bring to a boil. Add the mortar mixture and peas, then salt to taste. Continue the boil, stirring and rotating the pan occasionally until the rice is no longer soupy, but is covered with sufficient liquid to continue to cook the rice. Stir in the lump crabmeat (you can add the shells or crab parts at this time) and transfer the pan to the oven and cook, uncovered, until the rice is almost al dente (10-12 minutes)

Remove to a warm spot and cover with foil until the rice is cooked to taste (5-10 minutes).

TULANE CONTRIBUTOR

John Wallace (TUSA 1981)

Growing up in a family of doctors, I started Tulane University in Pre-Med in 1973, despite not having any reliable education in chemistry (a mandatory course for medicine at the time). After three semesters of the same course without advancement and on probation, I applied for and was accepted into TUSA. (Coincidentally, TUSA was housed in the old Tulane School of Medicine building). After graduating in 1981, I worked in several architectural offices in Texas and Louisiana. I transitioned into Project Management in 1983 when I joined the team assigned to oversee the construction of the 1984 Louisiana World Exposition. After the

Grand Opening of the Fair, I realized my passion was more about building buildings and less about designing them. The majority of my 39 years in business has been in Retail Development. I have had the great opportunity to build centers across the US, Canada, Spain, and Italy. To date, Debra and I have packed and unloaded our worldly possessions thirteen times for work. Over the years, and with the aid of the internet (non-existent when we started school), I have had the great joy of staying in touch with my TUSA classmates. I'm equally amazed at everyone's degrees of success.

MADRID XANADU (SHOPPING CENTER IN ARROYOMOLINOS, SPAIN) DESIGNED BY JOHN WALLACE

Gnocchi de Spinaci al Burro e Parmigiano

Spinach Gnocchi with Butter and Parmesan

2 CUPS BLANCHED SPINACH, CHOPPED AND SQUEEZED VERY DRY

1 CUP GRATED PARMESAN CHEESE

1 CUP FLOUR

1 CUP RICOTTA CHEESE

2 EGG YOKES

1 PINCH OF NUTMEG

8 TBSP UNSALTED BUTTER

Preheat your oven to 350 degrees.

Place spinach in a mixing bowl and 1/2 of the Parmesan cheese, 1/2 of the flour, all of the ricotta cheese, all of the egg yolks, a pinch of nutmeg, and salt and pepper to taste. Mix together until well blended.

With well-floured hands, shape the mixture into "sausage rolls" of about 1 1/4" diameter and roll them in the remaining 1/2 cup of flour. Cut the rolls into 1/2" segments, then shape them to about the size of a walnut.

Bring a pot of lightly salted water to a boil. Cook the gnocchi a few at a time and as they rise to the surface, transfer them into a colander with a slotted spoon. Transfer the drained gnocchi to a buttered baking dish but do NOT crowd them. Sprinkle with Parmesan cheese and heat in an oven at 350 degrees for about 20 minutes.

1.2 MILLION SQUARE FEET OF RETAIL AND ENTERTAINMENT FEATURING SPAIN'S ONLY INDOOR SKI FACILITY WITH A 250 METER RUN

Angiletti
Design Studio

KAMPALA, UGANDA
CURRENTLY PRACTICING

Sharon Sheltzer

TUSA 1980

TAICHUNG CULTURAL CENTRE, TAIWAN (ANGILETTI DESIGN STUDIO)

"With advanced 3D software and a highly creative team with experience from Europe, USA & East Africa, we try to push the boundaries of what can be done opting to ask why not! Nothing is impossible and the most complex of problems can be solved with the simplest of solutions.

Angiletti is now getting recognition as one of the leading contemporary design firms in East Africa with its bold and radical designs that are unconventional to the region. Angiletti's style and approach to design has seen the relatively young firm win several design competitions against the more well established companies.

The firm continues to inspire the industry, clients and generations both young and old that are fedup of stereotypical and sort-of-backward thinking of many people and professionals in the region."

-ANGILETTI DESIGN STUDIO

A.M. HOUSE IN BUWATTE, UGANDA (ANGILETTI DESIGN STUDIO)

Angiletti Design Studio | Recipes

MAIN COURSE
Colorful Pumpkin Stirfry

DRINK
Avocado Shake

Since this design firm is cutting edge in Uganda and disdains traditional and unimaginative approaches to building, I imagine they would be attracted to the recipes by Sophia Musoki from "A Kitchen in Uganda." She is the first food blogger in Uganda, and she features reimagined recipes with local ingredients. The following recipes are adapted from her blog.

- Sharon Sheltzer

GENESIS 120 CONDOMINIUMS IN NAALYA, UGANDA (ANGILETTI DESIGN STUDIO)

Avocado Shake

1 MEDIUM OVERRIPE AVOCADO

1/2 CUP MILK

3 TBSP HONEY

1 OVERRIPE BANANA

LIME FOR GARNISHING

Peel the avocado and banana and put in a blender. Add milk and honey and puree. Pour in a glass and garnish with lime.

Colorful Pumpkin Stirfry

1 CUP TENDER PUMPKIN,
THINLY SLICED

1 CUP CARROTS, JULIENNED

1/2 CUP GREEN PEPPER, JULIENNED

1/2 CUP GREEN BEANS, JULIENNED

1 LARGE ONION, THINLY SLICED

2 GARLIC CLOVES, FINELY CHOPPED

1/2 TSP GINGER, FINELY CHOPPED

1 TBSP SOY SAUCE DILUTED
WITH 2 TBSP WATER

BLACK PEPPER

A PINCH OF SUGAR

SALT

OIL

Place a pan on high heat. Add oil. Add the pinch of sugar and let it melt and turn slightly brown (but not burnt). Add garlic and ginger. Let it brown a little and then add the pumpkin. Keep stirring. After 3 minutes, add the green beans and keep stirring. Add the onions and carrots. Next add the green pepper. Keep stirring so they don't burn since the heat is high. Pour in the soy sauce little by little while continuing to stir until the vegetables are slightly tender. Sprinkle salt and pepper. Give one last stir before removing from fire and serve hot.

Both recipes adapted from Sophia Musoki's "A Kitchen in Uganda"

TULANE CONTRIBUTOR

Sharon Sheltzer (TUSA 1980)

Sharon never dreamed of being an architect. She just wanted to find a way to better the world; hence a Tulane Architecture thesis project featuring a college where green architecture was embodied and taught. Career energy was spent designing and building rammed earth, straw bale, and small homes. Special community projects include a Tiny Home Village for homeless persons in Visalia and latrines in Uganda. Fun tiny home projects include a treehouse in Visalia overlooking the Sierra Nevadas. Although remaining active in the community, she now spends more time kayaking, cooking, and writing.

FAVORITE RECIPE

Cioppino

MARINARA SAUCE

28 OZ. TOMATO PUREE

8 OZ. TOMATO PASTE

4 CLOVES GARLIC

1 ONION

1 TEASPOON OREGANO

1 TEASPOON SALT

1/2 TEASPOON PEPPER

1/2 TEASPOON RED PEPPER

1/2 CUP CHOPPED GREEN OLIVES

1/2 CUP RED WINE

1/3 CUP OF PARSLEY

SEAFOOD

SHRIMP

FISH CHUNKS

SCALLOPS

STEAMED CLAMS

CRAB LEGS

I'm known for my cioppino and I have tasted it all over the world looking for the best flavor. Here is a simple version with a secret ingredient (olives).

After cooking the sauce and resting it for one day in the refrigerator (for all spices to blend), add fish broth or concentrated clam base plus water and 1 cup white wine to the sauce. Bring to a low boil and add seafood for about 4 or 5 minutes cooking time. Serve in large bowls and sprinkle with chopped basil or parsley.

THE SOMMER TREEHOUSE, DESIGNED BY SHARON SHELTZER (PHOTOGRAPH BY FRANK MIRAMONTES, PUBLISHED IN LIFESTYLE MAGAZINE)
BELOW: ILLUSTRATION BY SHARON SHELTZER

Chicken Pot Pie
(Continued from page 143)

...until the cornmeal is sticking hard to the bottom of the skillet but not burning, about 2 to 3 minutes. Add 1 more cup of stock, scrape the bottom of the skillet, and bring the mixture to a simmer. Add the pearl onions, parsley, carrots, fried bacon, the remaining 2 cups of stock, and the remaining 3/4 teaspoon seasoning mix. Scrape the bottom and sides of the skillet and bring to a boil, reduce heat to low, and simmer until the mixture has thickened a little and the vegetables are barely tender, about 8 to 10 minutes. Remove from the heat.

Dice the cooled chicken breasts into 1/2-inch pieces. Stir the chicken into the skillet and then pour the mixture into a shallow pan. Refrigerate for about 30 minutes. Preheat the oven to 350 degrees.

TO FINISH, carefully divide the dough in half with the side of your hand. Sprinkle a clean surface lightly with flour. Flatten one piece of the dough with your hand and roll out the dough to a circle about 1/8 inch thick. Coat a deep pie or cake pan with cooking spray and line with the rolled-out dough. Roll out the remaining dough the same way. Fill the pie bottom with the cooled filling mixture and cover with the second round of dough. Seal the edges with the tines of a fork. Pierce the center of the top crust and bake until golden brown, 50 minutes to 1 hour. Cool 15 to 20 minutes. Cut into wedges and serve warm.

NOTE: To toast cornmeal, place the cornmeal (you need a total of 1 cup toasted yellow cornmeal for this recipe) in a small skillet over medium-high heat. Shake the pan and flip the cornmeal constantly until a light golden brown, about 4 minutes. Remove from the heat.

Adapted from Chef Paul Prudhomme's Seasoned America

Pickled Red Onions
(Continued from page 129)

(Continued from page 129)

1/2 RED ONION, THINLY SLICED

1/2 CUP WHITE OR APPLE CIDER VINEGAR (I LIKE THE BITE OF WHITE VINEGAR —ANDREA MAYHEW HANSON)

3/4 TEASPOON KOSHER SALT

1 1/2 TBSP SUGAR

1 TSP EACH, WHOLE CUMIN AND CORIANDER SEEDS

2 GARLIC CLOVES, CUT IN HALF

1/2 TSP DRIED MEXICAN OREGANO

Bring vinegar, water, salt, sugar, spices, and garlic to a boil. Lower heat and simmer for one minute, stirring to make sure the salt and sugar are dissolved. Place the onions in a glass container. Pour the mixture into the container and let stand until cool. Cover and store in refrigerator for up to 3 weeks.

Adapted from Sylvia Fountaine's food blog, "Feasting at Home"

As some point, John Wallace, Beth Ganser, and I decided the school needed a photo wall so that students could find each other. Here was my illustrated announcement of the photo session which hung over the steps going up to the studios from 1980.

- *Wellington "Duke" Reiter*

AFTERWORD

As I thumb through this remarkable volume assembled by my former classmates at the Tulane School of Architecture, I am struck by their passion for architecture, food, drink, and—most importantly—lasting comradery. For those of us who had the privilege of being part of this group, I am not sure we fully comprehended what a singular convergence of personalities, environment, and talents we were witnessing at the time…or that some 45 years later, the spirit of the class would still be in evidence as manifested in this book. With the advantage of lived experience, it is now possible to identify the key ingredients which bonded this unique set of future architects and thinkers:

• For many of us arriving from less exotic locales, New Orleans was a revelation. The easy availability of diverse cultures, foods, music, and indigenous architecture was unlike anything we had experienced previously. NOLA was an extension of the campus and we reveled in exploring and experiencing it together.

• Richardson Hall—the home of the school—was something akin to a big, well-worn, comforable house, not an institutional building. Symmetrically organized with a welcoming front door and enormous double-hung windows on all floors, it was a lantern glowing throughout the night and the attraction was irresistible.

• Architectural design was still an analog endeavor in the early 80's and did not have the portability our laptops allow today. Accordingly, the studio was more than a necessary place of work—it was social gathering space strewn with paper, books, and materials of all kinds as well as music, consumables, and often raucous conversation.

• And lastly, there was something special about the work itself. Unlike digital tools we rely on today which tend to homogenize output, the relatively primitive drawing and model-making equipment of the time allowed for a spectacular variation in individual expression and experimentation, something which was nurtured in the course of a special educational experience.

For those of us who know the backstory, all of the above is very much in evidence in this book. I hope something equally compelling comes through for readers, cooks, and travelers of all kinds. From my perspective, it is an unexpected pleasure to have such a vivid reminder of my fellow classmates and the joy they continue to find in their life journeys.

Wellington "Duke" Reiter, FAIA, TSA '81
Senior Advisor to the President, Arizona State University
Former Dean of the College of Design, ASU
Former President of the School of the Art Institute of Chicago

INDEX OF RECIPES

SALADS

Arugula with goat cheese, toasted
nuts, and fresh fruit 122
Simple French Salad 64
Waldorf Salad 109

SOUPS AND STEWS

Audrey's New England Fish
Chowder 42
Chesapeake Oyster Stew 49
Cioppino 166
Manhattan Clam Chowder 109
Potage Pintar 96
Pozole Verde 90
Red Lentil Soup 20
Sopa de Gato 153
Tomato Soup 146
Traditional Bahamian Stew Fish 65

VEGETARIAN

Colorful Pumpkin Stirfry 165
Confit Byaldi (Ratatouille) 79
Pisto Manchego a la Lancaster 155

DESSERTS

Bananas Foster 50
Caramel Cup Custard 141
Jericalla 91
No-Bake Skyr Cake 72
Oatmeal Chocolate Chip Butterscotch
Cookies 92
Pistachio Ice Cream 44
Pomegranate Gelato 29
Scarpagrappa Truffles 103
Six-Layer Tiramicarlo 102
Tarta de Santiago (Spanish almond
cake) with Gelato

DRINKS

Automne en Normandie 43
Basilisk Cocktail 130
Cadiz Collins 153
Cazuela 91
Chimay Gold Clone 16-17
Classic Mojito 56
Corbu Cocktail 79
The Creole Contentment 148
Ginger Rum César 124
Hibiscus Paloma 129
The Hemingway Daquiri 65
Mac Heard's Old Fashioned 147
Mimosa 134
New Orleans Milk Punch 48
Porto Tonico 158
Sazerac 51
Shots of Brinniven 71
Sidecar Cocktail 37
Sun Tea with Lemon 85
Syllabub 97

CREDITS

PHOTOS

12-14
Images courtesy of Wikimedia Commons

18-19, 23, 25
Images courtesy of Shutterstock

32-33, 40-41, 45-46, 52
Images courtesy of Wikimedia Commons

53
Image courtesy of Shutterstock

62
Image courtesy of Wikimedia Commons

65
Image courtesy of Unsplash.com

66
Image courtesy of Alpha Stock / Alamy Stock Photo

69
Image courtesy of Wikimedia Commons

69
Image courtesy of Unsplash.com

82-83, 88-89
Image courtesy of Wikimedia Commons

100-101
Image courtesy of Shutterstock

105
Image courtesy of Wikimedia Commons

106
Image courtesy of Unsplash.com

107
Images courtesy of Library of Congress

118-119, 122
Images sourced from https://pcparch.com/

126-127
Images courtesy of Wikimedia Commons

132-133
Images courtesy of NC Modernist

150-151
Images courtesy of Wikimedia Commons

156
Image courtesy of Wikimedia Commons

157
Image courtesy of Unsplash.com

158
Image courtesy of Wikimedia Commons

162-164
Images sourced from https://www.angiletti.com/

RECUPES

Lightning Source UK Ltd.
Milton Keynes UK
UKHW051209020621
384744UK00002B/100